PREFACE

Dance is an extraordinary display of physical skill that can convey both raw energy and charming delight. Chiseled poses, innovative choreography, and striking images are the hallmarks of the art form. As a dancer today, you are truly fortunate. The opportunities to perform in competitions, Broadway shows, and professional ballet companies readily exist if you are strong and talented. Dance represents impeccable balance, intense muscular control, grace, rhythm, and speed. What could be more exciting than to be chosen by the artistic director to perform a leading role? But you must be mentally and physically fit in order to compete in this high-performance market. The need to impress audiences has never been more evident; extreme choreography sells tickets and wins competitions.

Dance schools, studios, and academies are busy places. Classes, rehearsals, performances, and competition schedules are overwhelming. You are working harder than ever and doing your best to understand every correction given. Your instructors are inundated with teaching technique, musicality, and tricky choreography as well as marketing their business. Sometimes the details of technique class can get overlooked. Dance technique has been passed down over the years with very little anatomical analysis. This tradition might have worked for generations, but in order for you to have an edge over other dancers today, you must understand basic anatomy and receive the most proficient training.

Each combination at the barre and in the center must have a definitive purpose. The barre work is not just a series of pliés and tendus but an organization of your body. Technique class should emphasize the development of muscular strength to control and protect the joints. You need to understand the actions of the muscle groups that create the various combinations of dance positions. For example, the muscles that create extension of a joint must contract throughout the whole range. If you are not sure which muscles create the extension, how can you possibly execute that combination effectively? You will continue to overrecruit the wrong muscles, either building bulk or causing an overuse injury.

Dance Anatomy will assist you in discovering more efficient ways of improving technique. You will enhance your movements by knowing exactly which muscles contract to create the action. This book has more than 100 illustrations of exercises that give you a visual understanding of anatomy. You will see inside every tendu, passé, and arabesque to help you improve your lines.

Each chapter addresses a key principle of movement to help you improve performance. Chapter 1 is the foundation of the book; it highlights three beautiful positions of dance showing the entire body and the musculature. This chapter also emphasizes the importance of having a basic understanding of how your body works through descriptions of anatomy, movement planes, and muscular actions.

Chapters 2 through 8 have been organized moving through the body from the center out. Chapter 2 addresses spinal alignment and placement—where it all begins. The spinal curves and all movements of the spine are addressed. Specific exercises are devoted to placement of the spine. The exercises in this chapter are not meant to be challenging; they are meant to educate you on muscular awareness and its role in supporting the spine for better alignment.

Chapter 3 focuses on the anatomy of breathing. It's common for dancers to breathe with the upper chest, creating tension and early fatigue. The illustrations show how the diaphragm, the lungs, and the ribs work together to provide more oxygen to your body and improve stamina. The five exercises in this chapter emphasize the details of breathing during various movements; they are meant to encourage quality of upper-body movement and reduce upper-body tension.

Chapter 4 details the role of the core musculature in dance movement and presents exercises that develop strength in the core. The quadratus lumborum and the iliopsoas also work together with the abdominal layers to provide stability for the spine. A basic dance class might not address all layers of abdominal muscles and their importance in enhancing technique, so supplemental core conditioning work is almost always necessary for dancers.

Chapter 5 details the musculature of the shoulders and arms; the exercises will help you improve your port de bras and lifting skills. Chapter 6 focuses on strengthening the pelvis for optimal hip rotation. The exercises in chapter 7 focus on elegance and power of the legs.

The majority of dance injuries occur at the ankles and feet, so chapter 8 emphasizes conditioning for the lower legs. There are 26 bones and 34 joints in the foot, thus creating multiple movement possibilities. These small joints are responsible for weight transfer, push-off, and landings. Without sufficient strength in these joints, alignment and technique will be compromised. Chapter 8 has detailed exercises for strength, alignment, balance, and flexibility of the lower legs, ankles, and feet.

Chapter 9 presents exercises that involve multiple areas of the body. In addition to strengthening, these exercises promote your body's ability to work as a unit to accomplish your positions and movements.

To benefit from the exercises in this book, you must develop an effective conditioning program that takes into consideration your changing cycles of classes, practices, and times of layoff. This may be a whole new concept for you, but the goals here are to limit the volume of ineffective training and improve the quality of effective training. Planning a supplementary conditioning program to enhance your technique is discussed in chapter 1.

To progress as a dancer, you need to be organized and precise in the overall appearance of your movement. Your body must have definitive direction within the space that you are using. The various imaginary planes mentioned throughout *Dance Anatomy* can help you establish detail in your lines and make the execution of the choreography clear and concise. If your movement is clean, it will be more rhythmic and musical. Whether you are competing in front of a panel of judges, performing on stage, or taking a technique class, the judges, audiences, and instructors want to see power, clean lines, and a musical precision.

This book will answer your questions about achieving better turnout, a higher développé, a more flexible cambré, and a better arabesque. All of the exercises provide instruction on proper breathing techniques, education on recruiting the core muscles for improved placement, and important safety tips. The lists of muscles in the exercises are accompanied by detailed illustrations that highlight the muscles in the dance positions. You can actually see the relationship between the exercise and the dance position; this applies to all forms and styles of dance.

The exercises in *Dance Anatomy* will help you put more practical thought into your dance work without compromising the beauty of the art form. You can use this text as a tool for understanding corrections and the mechanics of your own body movements. You will benefit and continue the process of refining your physique and improving technique for that moment when the director picks you for the leading role!

ACKNOWLEDGMENTS

For Bob and my beautiful daughters, who, through their love and patience, teach me love and patience; for my beloved parents and one of my sisters who will never see this book, I'm sorry it took me so long; and for my other sweet sister, whose creativity and gentleness completes our family.

The dance medicine field has scores of talented health care professionals devoted to research and continuing education just for dancers. Their wisdom teaches me what I know today and what I will learn tomorrow.

We have different gifts according to the grace given us. If doing what you love is a gift, then I am blessed with gifts. My sincere gratitude to the many dancers I enjoyed working with during this process:

Adi Almeida, Ballet De Espana
Ally Garcia, McGing Irish Dancers
Andrea Lankester, North Carolina School of the Arts
Andrew Hubbard, Exhale Dance Tribe
Annie Honebrink, Otto M. Budig Academy of Cincinnati Ballet
Anthony Krutzkamp, Cincinnati Ballet
Bonita Brockert, National Dance Council of America
Calvin Thomas, Jr., Ballet Austin
Cervilio Miguel Amador, Cincinnati Ballet
Danielle Betscher, Just Off Broadway
Dawn Kelly, Cincinnati Ballet
Diamond Ancion, School for Creative and Performing Arts
Eugene Brockert, Dance, USA
Heather Walter, Wellington Orthopedics
Jill Marlow Krutzkamp, Cincinnati Ballet
Joseph Gatti, Ballet De Espana
Katie Chal, Louisville Ballet School
Kristi Capps, Cincinnati Ballet
Laura Tighe, McGing Irish Dancers
Marisa Gordon, Dance, Etc.
Zach Grubbs, Cincinnati Ballet

THE DANCER IN MOTION

Motion is defined as any physical movement or change in position. But, when you watch a dancer in motion, it is much more than physical changes in position. It is a vibrant visual art of brief images created by strength, balance, and grace. The aesthetics of this art form can never be sacrificed by scientific analysis. But learning basic movement principles will allow your body to move effectively and safely. We use illustrations of three dance positions— the jazz layout position, the attitude derrière position, and the split jump—to demonstrate movement principles in this chapter. These are shown in figures 1.1, 1.2, and 1.3.

Figure 1.1   The jazz layout position.

Figure 1.2   The attitude derrière position.

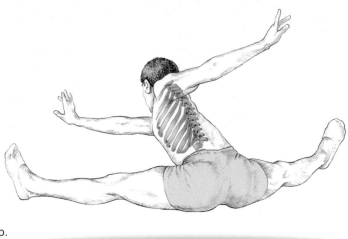

Figure 1.3
The split jump.

Bones, Joints, and Skeletal Muscles

To understand movement, you need to have a basic understanding of bones, joints, and muscles. They are the building blocks that provide you with the ability to create human motion. Your body is an amazing evolving gift of energy and information. Knowing how to organize the building blocks will give you fresh energy and enhance your skills as a dancer.

Bones

You have 206 bones in your body; they provide support and serve as levers for your muscles. Some bones provide protection for your internal organs, and some bones are responsible for producing red blood cells. You have long bones, short bones, and flat bones throughout your body that play a role in movement.

Movement operation involves the use of leverage. A lever is a rigid bar that moves a fixed point when effort, or force, is applied to it. The effort is used to move a resistance, or load. So, in your body, your joints are the fixed point, the bones are the levers, and the effort is the muscle contraction. For example, look at figure 1.1 of the jazz layout position. Focus on the gesture leg: The hip joint is the fixed point, the hip flexors are the effort by their contraction, and the femur (thigh bone) is the lever. Your muscles are attached to the bones by tendons, and the bones attach to each other by way of strong ligaments.

Joints

Joints are where two bones meet. You need to be familiar with several types of joints, but ball-and-socket, hinge, and gliding joints are the main types discussed in this text. All movement occurring at the joints have specific names, most working in pairs. The pairings typically describe movement in the same plane but work in opposite directions. For example, flexion at the knee would represent bending of the knee; extension at the knee would represent straightening of the knee (table 1.1).

The hip and shoulder joints are described as ball-and-socket joints. One end of the bone is rounded, and the end of its meeting bone is cup shaped. In the hip, for example, this is important information for improving turnout and développé; we explore this concept further in chapter 6. The hip joint has a deeper cup than the shallow shoulder joint. Look closely at figure 1.2—the standing (supporting) leg's hip joint shows how the femoral head fits into the acetabulum. Visualize how movement occurs at this joint; it has rotational action as well as flexion and extension.

Gliding joints are made up of bones in which both ends are relatively flat; they allow for very little movement. For example, the point where each rib meets the spinal vertebrae is a gliding joint, as in figure 1.3. Notice how there can be very little movement where the vertebrae and the ribs meet. This is significant for understanding the lack of good flexibility throughout the mid-spine (thoracic) region, which is covered more in chapter 2.

A hinge joint is a bone with a slight concave end meeting a bone with a convex end. The knee would be described as a hinge joint. When the knee flexes and extends, it allows movement primarily in one plane. As you will learn later in this text, the knee does have a slight rotational movement as well. But focus on figure 1.1—the supporting leg is showing flexion of the knee while the gesture leg is showing extension of the knee.

Table 1.1 Joint Movements

Action	Movement	Example
Flexion	Bending, folding of a joint	Hip flexion: front of hip bends with grande battement devant
Extension	Straightening of a joint	Elbow straightens when in a push-up position
Abduction	Moving away from center	Arms in à la seconde: moving from alongside the body to second position
Adduction	Moving toward center	Assemblé: legs coming together
External rotation	Rotating outward	Turnout: grande plié in second position
Internal rotation	Rotating inward	Shoulder joint internally rotates to place the hand on the hip
Plantar flexion	Pointing the foot	Relevé, en pointe
Dorsiflexion	Flexing the foot	Rocking back on heels, lifting forefoot

Skeletal Muscles

Skeletal muscles initiate skeletal movement; they are composed of connective tissue partitions containing muscle cells, fibers, and numerous nerves. When the nerves are stimulated by your brain, a chemical reaction occurs, causing the muscle to contract. Each muscle has an origination point on a bone and an insertion point on a bone. Basically, on contraction, the muscle fibers shorten and have a tendency to pull both ends into the middle.

How muscles react to stimuli depends on their characteristics. There are basically two types of fibers in each muscle: slow twitch, or type I, and fast twitch, or type II. Slow-twitch fibers contract slowly and have a high resistance to fatigue. They are used primarily for placement and posture as well as aerobic activities. The fast-twitch fibers contract quicker and have a low resistance to fatigue. They can produce more power than slow-twitch fibers. Petit allegro, or short anaerobic movements, use primarily fast-twitch fibers. Most ballet dancers have a higher percentage of slow-twitch fibers, while dancers who have a more muscular or bulky look will have a higher percentage of fast-twitch fibers. No matter what your dance intensity level is, the slow-twitch fibers will be recruited first, followed by fast-twitch fibers.

All of your muscles have the capability of contracting, or creating tension, in various ways. Dynamic contraction is described as any type of tension on a muscle where the length of the muscle changes. This would certainly create movement at the joint. The two types of dynamic contractions are concentric and eccentric. Concentric contraction is typically a shortening of a muscle to create the movement, and eccentric contractions involve lengthening of the muscle. During pointe tendu, as the leg moves away from your center and your foot points, the calf muscles shorten, creating a concentric contraction. As your foot returns to the starting position, the calf muscles begin to lengthen. During that return phase, the calf muscles work eccentrically. The significance of this comes into play especially when landing from jumps. The eccentric contraction of the muscles will help to decelerate your body against gravity on landing. While you work so hard to build strength and power to jump higher, you also need to work on control to reduce the risk of injury and to make your return phase smooth and coordinated.

Another type of contraction that creates tension on the muscle but does not change the length is an isometric (also called static) contraction. An isometric contraction means equal length—the muscle fires, creating tension, but there is no joint movement. So, as you execute a relevé in first position and hold, the hold phase is an isometric contraction of all of the muscles in the legs. They contract concentrically to elevate you and then hold isometrically.

As your muscles contract to produce movement, various muscles work together to achieve the goal. All dance movements are carefully controlled because the muscles work so well together. Skeletal muscles are divided into four distinct categories: agonists, antagonists, synergists, and stabilizers.

• **Agonists.** The muscles that contract to produce the movement are the movers, or agonists. The ones that are the most effective in making that movement happen are the primary movers. For example, the action of pointing your foot is created by the gastrocnemius and soleus muscles as the primary movers, but other muscles, called the secondary movers, assist.

- **Antagonists.** The muscles that oppose the primary movers are called antagonists. They somewhat relax and lengthen while the prime movers are working, but other times they can contract with the prime movers and provide a cocontraction. Now, as you might imagine, the agonists and the antagonists are located opposite of each other. Look at figure 1.2, and focus on the gesture leg in attitude derrière. The agonists are the hamstring and gluteal muscles that activate to move the leg to the back into hip extension. The antagonists are the hip flexors, or the muscles along the front of the hip and thigh. They are on a stretch while the movers contract. Now, imagine a grande plié in second position. As you are coming up, the quadriceps (agonists) are working to straighten the knee, but the hamstrings (antagonists) can contract as well, providing a cocontraction and better support for your knee joint.

- **Synergists.** Synergist muscles can be confusing, so let's break things down. Muscles that are considered synergists have two functions: They can promote the movement or they can neutralize the movement. What is so important for you to know is that the synergist muscles fire to help you define your movement. They can counteract any unwanted directional force. So, in figure 1.2, focus on the right arm. When you forcefully lift your arm by flexing at the shoulder joint, what helps to keep the humerus (upper arm) bone from separating away from the scapula (shoulder blade)? A small muscle hidden under the pectoralis major called the coracobrachialis displays synergistic qualities by contracting to assist in controlling the movement of the humerus in relation to the scapula. Although the primary movers get all the credit, the synergists help the agonists with establishing smooth and coordinated movement.

- **Stabilizers.** Muscles that are able to fixate a joint are called stabilizers. This is important and will be reviewed repeatedly throughout this book and its exercises. Stabilizers serve as anchors; they are able to hold a joint firm in order for other movement to occur. In figure 1.2, what is holding the spine stable? The abdominals are contracting to stabilize the spine; without that contraction, the momentum and strength of the gesture leg moving backward would cause the spine to collapse. You are working so hard on the leg that is creating most of the movement that you forget about the importance of the muscles that create stability and hold you firm in order for that movement to occur.

Movement Planes

Motion means changes in position; motion is created by force. For you, the coordinated efforts of body and mind create the force. So, let's begin by focusing on the efforts of your body and become familiar with some anatomical positions that are used in the text. When a muscle contracts, it produces movement at the joint, and the joint is the connector between the bones—easy enough, right? Dance moves you in all different directions, patterns, and shapes.

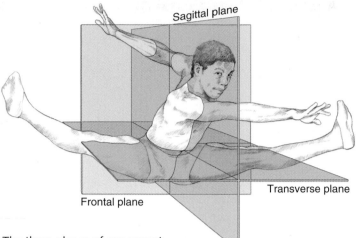

Figure 1.4   The three planes of movement.

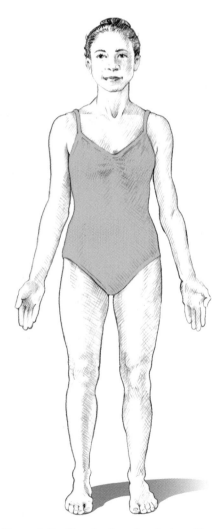

Figure 1.5   Standard anatomical position.

You can better understand these movements by dividing the body into three imaginary planes: frontal (vertical), sagittal, and transverse (horizontal), which will be described soon. Learning challenging choreography and executing the movement with beautiful lines come from a better understanding of how your body moves in space. Look at figure 1.4 showing these three planes within your body. These planes correspond to three dimensions in space.

Now, because you can change your orientation within space and your arms and legs can change position, it's important to organize positional directions of movement and refer to your body in a standard anatomical position, as in figure 1.5. That position is facing front, feet comfortably parallel, arms by your sides, and the palms of your hands rotated to face front. From this position, all directional body movements can begin from a starting point and all anatomical terminology has a starting point (table 1.2).

Table 1.2 Anatomical Position and Directional Terminology

Term	Definition
POSITIONAL TERMINOLOGY	
Anatomical position	Standing with feet and palms facing front
Supine	Lying on the back
Prone	Lying facedown
DIRECTIONAL TERMINOLOGY	
Superior	Above or toward head
Inferior	Below or toward feet
Anterior	Front side or in front of
Posterior	Back side or in back of
Medial	Closer to the median plane or toward midline
Lateral	Farther from the median plane or toward side
Proximal	Closer to root of limb, trunk, or center of body
Distal	Farther from root of limb, trunk, or center of body
Superficial	Closer to or on surface of body
Deep	Farther from surface of body
Palmar	Anterior aspect of hand in anatomical position
Dorsal (for hands or feet)	Posterior aspect of hand in anatomical position; top aspect of foot when standing in anatomical position
Plantar	Bottom aspect of foot when standing in anatomical position

Reprinted, by permission, from K. Clippinger, 2007, *Dance anatomy and kinesiology* (Champaign, IL: Human Kinetics), 18.

Now, continue to visualize your standard anatomical position with various imaginary planes within yourself. You are divided into upper and lower halves by a transverse plane, equal right and left portions by a sagittal plane, and front and back portions by a frontal plane. So, for example, when moving your arms from en bas through first to high fifth position, you are moving within your sagittal plane. That movement has a purpose—it's working within an imaginary plane to high fifth efficiently, with no deviation and with no incorporation of other movement. When you cambré to the side, you are moving in the frontal plane, moving directly to the side without any other inefficient movement, as if you are side bending along an imaginary pane of glass. In various hip-hop movements, the hips rotate in and out—that movement describes each hip moving along the transverse plane. The same would apply when twisting from the waist: Your trunk moves along the transverse plane. Look at figure 1.3, the split jump.

In which plane are the legs moving? The frontal plane. If one leg were slightly more forward, the movement would not produce the clean line that you strive for. You would need to continue to repeat that split jump until you got it correct. The repetition and overrehearsing due to lack of understanding of where the legs should be could lead to an overuse injury.

Mindful Connections

Your mind plays an intense role in dance anatomy and improvement in technique. Imagining moving faster or lifting your legs higher is part of being a dancer in motion as well as understanding primary muscle movement. Visualization can also be a tool for helping you dance more effectively. How many times do you practice the act of développé? How many times do you feel gripping in the thigh and anxiety because you are unable to raise the leg higher? Imagine what it would be like to know which muscles need to contract, lengthen, and stabilize without gripping. Imagine your leg elevating higher without anxiety. This is using your mind along with physical ability.

Visualization

Visualization, imagery, and *mental simulation* are terms used to describe creating a picture in your mind without doing the physical activity. There are many kinds of imagery, but for this text let's focus on basic visualization skills to improve performance. You can use simple positive images and focus on maintaining a calm center to release unwanted tension. Visualize exactly what you want your body to do and keep your thoughts positive. Eric Franklin is a master at visualization; I love his term *seed imagery*—planting an intuitive thought and letting that image grow to increase performance. When you repeatedly train your actions (as you do in class and rehearsal), you induce physiological changes and increase accuracy. Take a little time every day to find a quiet spot, close your eyes, and just listen to yourself breathe. Now, imagine the dancer you want to be, and see yourself moving with ease. Focus on how clean your lines are. Continue to visualize how much control you have with every combination you perform. You can see it in your mind, you can hear the music playing, and you can feel your body executing the sequences with detail. Now, all you have to do is *do* it! Let everything else go, and focus on your technique. You are training the relationship between your mind and your muscles. They must work together to help you reach your goals.

Tension Relief

Your state of mind will definitely influence the outcome of your work. If you prepare for a pirouette with tension in the upper body, stress about having to execute two, and anxiety about losing your balance, how on earth can you turn? Visualize beautiful multiple turns around a firm but calm center and breathe! Dance your way into the pirouette, enjoy turning, release the fear, use rhythm to help you, and *turn*!

Research continues to look at the proven connection between stress and injury. You seek perfection and you push yourself beyond your limits. Dance, like any other sport, requires intense levels of training and conditioning to maintain the highest level of physical performance. When you allow competition anxiety or fear of failure to overwhelm your mind, you lose the ability to cope, and you put yourself at risk of getting hurt. When you can't maintain motivation, you create disruptions in attention, lose momentary awareness, and put yourself at risk for an acute injury. All of these stressors can also lead to hesitation, weakness in balance skills, and unwanted muscle tension.

The best dancers keep a healthy, positive conversation going within themselves to create motivation and encouragement. This inner dialogue can reduce tension and create an ease in your movement. Remember, you are building a healthy connection between mind and body. Accept yourself and love dancing—it's that easy! Be firm and tell yourself that it's possible. Unfortunately, you might be full of criticism and doubt; if you love to dance and want to improve, you must stop the negativity and dissatisfaction with yourself. Stay away from telling yourself you cannot do something or that some movement is too hard.

Dance-Focused Exercise

There is a distinct relationship between each exercise and the illustrations in these chapters. Throughout the exercises, visualize ease and balance in your neck as well as stability throughout your center, and allow those skills to carry over in your technique. For example, when performing the exercises for your legs, visualize ample joint mobility, not tension, in your hips. Remember to keep the images positive and brief. After practicing visualization skills during the exercises, send those brief images through your mind before classes, rehearsals, and performances. Notice how your skills improve; notice how you work more effectively with less gripping in your muscles. Keep using positive visualization skills. They are exercises of the mind and they require practice. Don't let negative thoughts creep back in and ruin your technique. Each chapter has a section called Dance-Focused Exercise guiding you on applying these skills to the exercises in that chapter.

Cardiorespiratory Benefits

Although dance-specific exercises are the focus of this book, the benefits of cardiorespiratory fitness cannot be overlooked. More and more medical research on dance documents that dancers' cardiorespiratory capacities are similar to the capacities of other athletes in nonendurance sports. Rehearsals and performances last for only brief periods; this type of exercise is referred to as anaerobic training. Aerobic training is required for improving cardiorespiratory health because it improves blood circulation and the supply of oxygen to the cells. Aerobic training increases heart size, which allows a larger volume of blood to be pumped through the body. Cardiorespiratory fitness allows for better transportation of oxygen and an increase in endurance levels. High cardiorespiratory endurance reduces physical and mental fatigue, which can also lead to injury. You can improve your cardiorespiratory endurance by training on an elliptical machine, treadmill, or stationary bike or swimming three or four times a week.

Conditioning Principles

You should be familiar with some principles in order to define and enhance your conditioning plan. Not only are you improving muscular strength, but you are also increasing strength in the tendons and ligaments.

• **Principle of overload.** If you want to increase strength, you must continue to work the targeted muscle group past your normal load. The exercises are executed at maximal contraction throughout the entire range of motion. Typically, this type of training uses fewer repetitions and more resistance, and it works your muscles to fatigue.

• **Principle of reversibility.** This refers to the fast loss of strength when the conditioning stops. In order to maintain your fitness level, continue with dance-specific conditioning at least four times a week if you are not dancing because of a layoff or holiday break. (Conditioning takes the form of the exercises presented in this book.)

• **Principle of specificity.** This relates to conditioning the dance-specific muscles that you need for improving your technique. In order for conditioning to be effective for dance, you must target and engage the muscles needed for dance as if your exercises were a dance!

• **Alignment.** All repetitions must be repeated without sacrificing alignment, core control, or proper breathing. Your goal is to work effectively. If you feel your alignment beginning to falter, stop, reorganize, and then start again. As you perform each exercise, emphasize the main muscle movement but notice how it affects your entire body.

• **Warm-up and cool-down.** Each conditioning session should begin with a basic warm-up to increase blood flow, accelerate your breathing, and slightly raise body temperature. The exercises will be more effective if you are warmed up. Take 10 minutes to include the exercises from chapter 2 to get centered and then add some low-level jogging in place. A sufficient cool-down after conditioning allows the body to return to its resting state. This can be approximately 10 minutes and can include the breathing exercises from chapter 3. You can also include some gentle stretching, which will reduce muscle soreness.

Each exercise has a specific goal, but all exercises require control through the full range of the movement. Avoid initiating the movement with your momentum and then allowing gravity or loss of awareness to finish the movement. Begin each exercise with slow, precise control and maintain that control through the exercise.

Your warm-up, cool-down, and exercise program should take approximately 50 minutes. Each chapter allows you to work with specific muscle groups to enhance the intensity and deepen your awareness. Keep your mind focused on safe skeletal alignment, which is emphasized throughout this book.

Agreeing on a conditioning program with specific durations, repetitions, sets, and intensities is next to impossible because opinions vary among the experts. For the purpose of this text, repeat each exercise 10 to 12 times for three sets, unless otherwise stated. But, this may require some practice to determine your personal needs. If you are trying to build strength, you must execute maximal muscle contraction through the entire range of motion and overload the muscle in a progressive manner. Some of the exercises in this book use resistance bands or small weights for progressive resistance, but the goal is to maintain excellent alignment. You can slowly add resistance when the alignment is secure and the exercise is no longer challenging. Quality of movement is the emphasis.

Your spine is able to create multidirectional movement that gives you the ability to execute various dance styles with fluidity and ease. Your spine can portray a resilient elastic look that might be needed for various contemporary combinations, or it can have a rigid and more stable, but elegant, look for partnering skills. Ballet posture may call for your spine to be strong but display a majestic and lifted look. It all depends on placement, balance, and organization of the muscle contractions. To improve body placement, you need a healthy balance of muscle action to support proper alignment of your spine. This chapter introduces muscles associated with optimal placement of the spine. Dance can put an enormous amount of stress on your back, especially in the segments that have the most mobility. Learning to use the entire spine and balance stability and flexibility can improve your performance skills and reduce your risk of injury.

Your axial skeleton is made up of the skull, spinal column, ribs, and sacrum. In anatomy, axial refers to anatomical direction; in the skeletal system it refers to your bones being aligned vertically along a longitudinal axis. What you need to remember is to move against the resistance of gravity, meaning that you need to create length, or axial elongation, within your spine while incorporating stability around the spine for placement and support.

Spinal Column

Your spine is a column of 33 strong bones called vertebrae that connect the skull, shoulders, ribs, hips, and legs; it is the center of your skeleton. The vertebrae also surround and protect the spinal cord, which transmits the impulses that control all voluntary and involuntary movements. The vertebrae are connected by small, fluid-filled sacks of tough, fibrous cartilage called discs, which allow for vertebral support as well as a small amount of cushioning. The discs help to absorb shock, especially when you perform jumping and lifting movements. The combined movement between all of the vertebrae creates the flexibility through the spine as a whole. While a large cambré (back-bend) type movement can be gorgeous, the tendency is to overextend in the neck and the lower back without trying to incorporate any effective movement through the thoracic spine (midback). Transmitting forces equally will allow the entire spine to work for you. Using only the neck or lower back will cause added physical stress in those specific areas and eventually tighten and weaken the rest of the spine. This is particularly significant in the lower back; if forces like gravity and compression are transmitted only through the lower spine, then you overwork that portion of your spine, putting yourself at serious risk for fractures, soft tissue damage, and disc degeneration.

The vertebrae cannot stand upright alone; they are supported by an elaborate system of ligaments. The major connecting ligaments are the anterior and posterior longitudinal ligaments. These ligaments are continuous bands that run down the front and back of the spine. Basically, all vertebrae have common structural patterns: a body, the vertebral foramen, a spinous process, and two transverse processes (figure 2.1). The body area of the vertebrae bears the weight of the body above it, the foramen creates the space for the spinal cord, and the processes are sites for various muscle and ligament attachments. The point at which each process meets the next process creates a gliding joint called a facet. At these small joints the vertebral processes are flat and each surface must slide smoothly against the other when you twist or bend. Injury to these small facet joints is usually produced by repetitive, uncontrolled movements that create asymmetry. When these small joints do not glide smoothly, your movement becomes limited and rigid. This causes pain and eventual compensations. While executing the upcoming exercises, visualize this smooth sliding effect between all vertebrae and incorporate it with control.

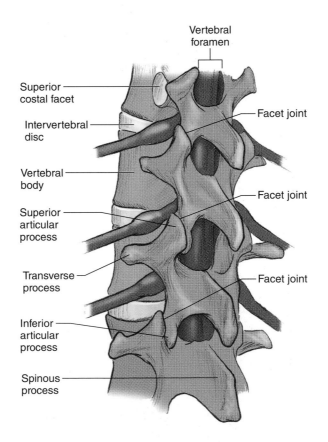

Figure 2.1   The structure of the vertebrae.

Spinal Regions

Your spine has three main sections: the cervical area, the thoracic area, and the lumbar spine and sacrum. Take a moment to notice all of the regions in the spine in figure 2.2 and how the vertebrae stack up so neatly. Excellent spinal health is dependent on maintaining the gentle, natural curves designed for balance and postural stability.

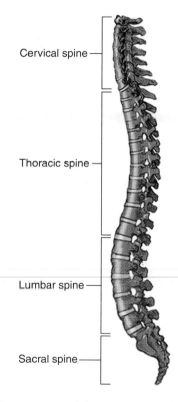

Cervical spine

Thoracic spine

Lumbar spine

Sacral spine

Figure 2.2   The three regions of the spine: cervical, thoracic, and lumbar and sacral regions.

Cervical Spine

The neck, or cervical spine, has seven vertebrae, along with ligaments, tendons, and muscles. It supports your head, which can weigh approximately 14 pounds (about 6 kg). The cervical vertebrae are labeled as C1 through C7. The neck area is relatively flexible and fragile because the vertebrae are slightly smaller than other vertebrae. The first two vertebrae are quite interesting. C1 is called the atlas (Atlas supporting the heavens from Greek mythology); it is literally a bony ring that is responsible for carrying the skull. C2 is called the axis; it has a small, bony projection that rises into the ring of C1, thus creating a pivot for rotation to occur between the atlas and axis. This creates movement for nodding and rotating the head. Physical tension throughout the cervical spine can limit efficient movement for spotting during turning. Think about your head being centered and balanced on top of C1 and C2. If your head is balanced, the neck muscles that control the movement can work with ease. Any time your head moves outside of this balanced state, the opposing muscles of that movement are responsible for overworking to try to maintain alignment. Head placement is an important addition to the aesthetics of all upper-body poses and choreography.

Thoracic Spine

As you continue down the spine, the size of the vertebrae increases. The thoracic spine contains 12 large vertebrae, T1 through T12. The ribs have attachments along the sides of the vertebrae in this region. The increasing size of the vertebrae with the added attachments of the ribs creates the lack of flexibility and mobility in this area, notably called the thoracic cage or rib cage. The principle of executing movement along the entire spine will continue to create mobility throughout the thoracic region. All of the exercises in this chapter are designed for you to focus on axial elongation in all movement planes, moving in the longest possible arc.

Lumbar Spine and Sacrum

Your lumbar, or lower-back, region has five vertebrae (L1 to L5) and is a more flexible area in comparison to the thoracic region. This region takes on the most stress. It is important to remember that the lower segments of the spinal column have the ability to move more in extension than rotation, which can create a shear force—meaning the vertebrae can slide in an anterior and posterior pattern, creating an unnecessary excessive sliding or shearing-type motion. This unsupported movement can eventually wear down the discs and cause weakness in the ligaments, significantly increasing your risk of lower-back injury. Basic spine education, awareness of body placement, and the ability to apply abdominal strengthening work to your spinal movements will reduce the risk of lower-back injuries.

There is also greater movement between the last vertebra and the sacrum. The sacrum is triangular in shape and is composed of five fused vertebrae (S1 to S5). It takes on the load of the upper body, transferring it to the pelvic girdle. Knowing that the lower spine has more flexibility in extension and takes on more of the load, you must understand the benefits of core and lower-back strengthening to improve your body placement and reduce the risk of injury. We introduce the importance of the core musculature in the upcoming Neutral Spine section, but we will discuss this principle in more detail in chapter 4.

Muscular Balance

This section introduces the muscles that play a role in correct placement of the spine, and we continue to elaborate on them throughout the rest of the text. The primary muscles along the front of the spine are the rectus abdominis, which runs from ribs 2 to 5 to the pubic bone, and the internal and external obliques, which also connect your ribs to your pelvis. The deepest of the abdominals is the transversus abdominis, which is primarily a postural muscle and very important for spinal stability. The deep transversus abdominis connects the lower ribs 7 through 12 with the pelvis; its fibers run horizontally. Another muscle associated with spinal placement is the iliopsoas muscle; it has a direct connection with your lower spine, pelvis, and femur (thigh) bone. Weakness or tightness of the iliopsoas can create instability in the lower region of your spine. (This muscle will be discussed further in chapter 6.) The hip flexor isometrics exercise on page 26 helps you locate and contract this muscle without causing instability in your lower back.

The posterior aspect of the spine is supported by the sacrospinalis (also known as erector spinae) and the deeper multifidi muscles, which run from the pelvis to the base of the skull. The deep multifidi muscles are also extremely important for improving body placement—on contraction they provide trunk control and spinal stability by providing gentle compression along the spine.

At this point, we introduce the pelvic floor of the body, which provides a strong base of support for the lower spine and pelvis. While more discussion on this follows in chapter 3, note that the pelvic floor attaches at the base of the pelvis and sacrum, which is located at the bottom of your spine. The ischial squeeze exercise on page 30 educates you on engaging these muscles and using them for improved placement.

Along the sides of the trunk are the quadratus lumborum muscles running from the last rib to the iliac rim and the lower spine along its way. This muscle helps you side bend and extend your lower back, but when it is tight it can elevate the pelvis or cause hip hike, especially with high kicking-type movements. A healthy balance of strength and flexibility along all sides of the spine provides the needed support for attaining well-aligned body placement.

Neutral Spine

Your spine is capable of flexion, extension, side bending, rotation, and various combinations of all of these movements, thus giving you the ability to perform any type of choreography. Four curves within the sagittal plane play a significant role in body placement (figure 2.3). In the cervical and lumbar areas, the curve is concave (it moves in a forward motion), whereas the thoracic and sacral curves are convex (they move in the opposite direction). Your intervertebral discs cushion your vertebrae within these curves. Changing the curves as a base for your placement causes undue stress on the discs and unnecessary muscle activity to maintain this misalignment.

Excellent body placement skills come from creating strength and stability along the spine while keeping the natural curves intact. This is known as neutral posture, neutral spine, or neutral pelvis. Dancing with axial elongation while maintaining the natural, neutral curves creates less stress on the discs and vertebrae. You know that challenging choreography requires you to move your spine in all directions and combinations of all directions, but a strong dancer can control the spine through the challenging movements. The locating neutral exercise on page 20 is focused on assisting you in locating the natural neutral pelvis position.

In looking at your body from the side, you should be able to draw an imaginary line from the middle of the ear down to the lateral malleolus, or

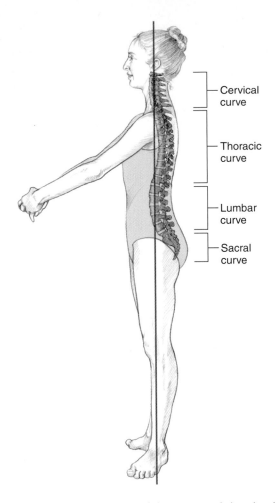

Cervical curve

Thoracic curve

Lumbar curve

Sacral curve

Figure 2.3   The four curves of the spine and the plumb line.

ankle bone, without any deviation. This is called a plumb line (figure 2.3). As the plumb line passes down, it would move through the center of the shoulder, through the center of the greater trochanter at the hip, and down to the knee. From there, the plumb line would continue to the lateral malleolus, again with no deviations. You should also be able to secure this alignment with the legs parallel or turned out.

Unfortunately, some dancers have difficulty maintaining a neutral or natural position of the lower back. The lumbar spine might slightly extend, creating lordosis (an excessive curve in extension). There are various reasons for lumbar lordosis. One is abdominal weakness, which leaves the lower spine unsupported, causing the lower back to arch. Another reason could be that the posterior spinal muscles are tight and short, which pulls the lower spine into an arched position. Or the iliopsoas muscles are tight and short, which also pulls the lumbar spine into this lordotic position.

Dance-Focused Exercise

While executing the following series of exercises, remember to work with axial elongation. It is important to let the cervical spine be an extension of the thoracic spine. For example, the exercises that involve flexion of the spine should allow the cervical spine to finish the arch that the midback has initiated. Look at trunk curl isometrics on page 24. There should not be an excessive bend in the neck to try to force the upper back to move more. The same principle of axial elongation comes into play when the spine is required to move into extension. The neck should be a beautiful continuation of the arch that the midspine is creating.

Now, take a look at the neutral spine model and notice how the spine stacks up; be aware of your alignment. The gentle curves of the spine are intact and supported. The head balances on top of the cervical spine with ease. Notice the balance between the muscles along the front and back of the spine. Think about how the deep multifidi gently compress your spine to give support. The quadratus lumborum situated on both sides of the lower spine keeps a healthy balance between the ribs and the pelvis. If you can visualize the iliopsoas connecting the lower spine to the thighs and the pelvic floor activating to stabilize the base of the spine, you have begun to develop improved placement. By incorporating balance, you actually will need less overall muscle action and have created an excellent workplace in which your spine can function.

Locating Neutral

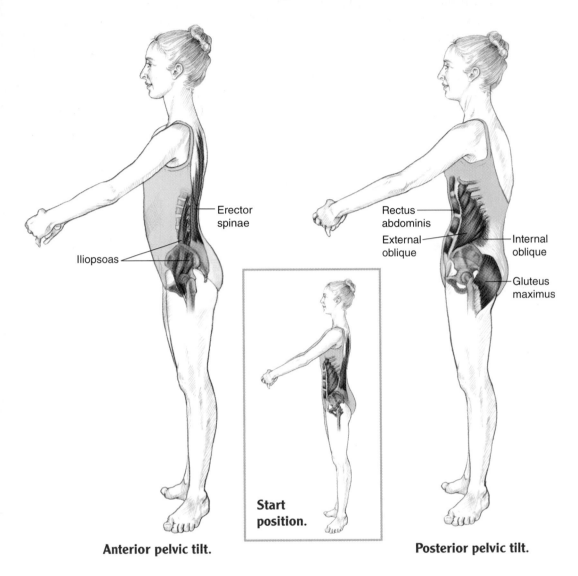

Erector spinae

Iliopsoas

Rectus abdominis

External oblique

Internal oblique

Gluteus maximus

Start position.

Anterior pelvic tilt.

Posterior pelvic tilt.

Execution

1. Begin by standing with legs and arms in first position. Create a lifted quality through your spine; gently engage the low abdomen and visualize the plumb line.

2. As you inhale, lift the ribs, release your abdominals, and gently rock the front of your pelvis forward, arching the lower back and moving into an anterior tilt. Notice the tightness in the upper and lower back and the looseness in your abdominals.

3. As you begin to exhale, reverse the tilt and tighten through the abdominals; try to flatten the lower back and engage the gluteus maximus. Notice how the front of the hips tightens and how the front of your chest drops.

4. Now return to a neutral position, visualizing the plumb line and gently lifting through your waist. There is balance between the abdominals and the spinal muscles and a renewed lengthened feeling in the spine.

5. Now, as you inhale, move into your anterior pelvic tilt. As you exhale, move into your neutral position. Emphasize abdominal contraction and the external obliques to move into neutral. Repeat this 10 to 12 times.

Muscles Involved

Anterior pelvic tilt: Iliopsoas, erector spinae

Posterior pelvic tilt: Rectus abdominis, internal oblique, external oblique, gluteus maximus

Dance Focus

Let this exercise help you work through your center and notice the changes that occur along your spine. In knowing that the lower portion of your spine has more flexibility, you must be aware of activating the abdominal muscles to have control of your pelvis and spine in a more natural, neutral position. Instructors can look for the anterior iliac bones and pubic bone aligned along the frontal plane and know that every dancer has different natural curves along the spine; the contraction of the abdominals helps to maintain and support the curves. Visualize how the external oblique musculature connects the ribs and the pelvis. Keep that connection working when your leg needs to move 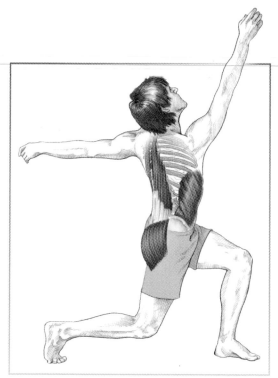 to the back—this will help to keep your pelvis and lower back from overextending. All styles require three-dimensional hip and pelvic movement, but control of those movements is one of the keys to technical improvement.

Leg Glide

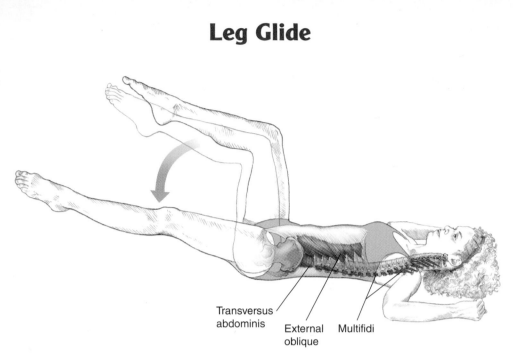

Transversus abdominis

External oblique

Multifidi

Execution

1. Lie on your back with arms in first position. (Note: In the illustration, the arms are placed in a position to make viewing the abdominals more visible.) Locate your neutral pelvic alignment and bring one leg at a time to 90-degree hip flexion and 90-degree knee flexion (90/90). Align your knees with your hips.

2. Inhale to prepare. As you breathe out, deepen the abdominal contraction and let one leg glide away from you at approximately 60 degrees. Allow your knee to fully extend. Focus on anchoring your abdominals to your lower back and allow no movement of the pelvis. Feel the deep transversus abdominis and external obliques firing to help stabilize your pelvis.

3. Inhale to bring the leg back to your starting position. Repeat the sequence with the other leg. As you exhale, focus on flattening your abdomen to anchor your pelvis; reemphasize deep abdominal contraction, not the hip flexors. Practice this 10 to 12 times on each leg.

4. As your leg moves away from your center to extend the knee, notice the movement of your legs occurring along your sagittal plane and actively increase the abdominal contraction to resist pelvic movement.

⚠ **SAFETY TIP** Maintain stability in your lower back. If you find that it is too difficult to hold your lower back in a stable neutral position, do not take the legs as low; try it again with the legs extending higher. You may lower the legs when your back is stable.

Muscles Involved

Transversus abdominis, external oblique, multifidi

Dance Focus

This exercise emphasizes the point that it is not about how many abdominal exercises you can perform; it's about using the strength of the abdomen to improve your technique. Irish dance requires intense trunk control in a neutral position in order to maintain a stable position. Focus on the deep transversus abdominis along with the deep multifidi to give you double support. This is a cocontraction, the anchor you need before all arm and leg motion. Remind yourself that only your legs are moving, not your pelvis or your spine! That same principle applies to jumping combinations. Visualize your navel moving toward your spine for added support; put your energy into your abdominal muscles, not tension into your neck and shoulders. Take a moment to practice a few small jumps in place. Feel the core muscles bracing your spine, and feel the external obliques working to connect your ribs and your pelvis. Relax and enjoy the ride! For teachers, this is a tool to help students move from their centers with less stress to their spines. Instructors must be able to feel it, explain it, and teach it.

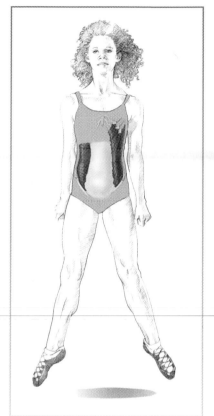

VARIATION

Rotated Leg Glide

1. Begin with your legs at 90/90, and turn out both thighs.

2. On exhalation, again deepen the abdominal contraction and lower one leg to approximately 60 degrees as you extend your knee. Maintain turnout and reemphasize leg movement only, not pelvis or spinal movement.

3. Inhale on the return, and focus on deepening the abdominal contraction while maintaining hip turn-out. Repeat this exercise 10 to 12 times on each leg.

Trunk Curl Isometrics

Rectus
abdominis

Execution

1. Lie on your back with knees bent and feet flat on the floor and arms by your sides. Inhale on the preparation and exhale as you engage the rectus abdominis to curl your trunk until the bottom edges of the shoulder blades lift off the floor. Gently glide the chin toward your Adam's apple, and allow your arms to reach for the backs of your thighs.

2. Place your hands behind your thighs and hold an isometric contraction. Emphasize moving the entire thoracic spine into a curl, and allow the spinal muscles to support that curling effect. Keep the sacrum firm on the floor; do not use the hip flexors.

3. Hold this position and feel the strength of the abdomen. With control, breathe in and slowly return to the floor, emphasizing the eccentric contraction of the rectus abdominis. Move along your sagittal plane, curling as much as possible through your upper back on the way up and uncurling on the way down. Work with control. Count to 4 for each action; repeat 10 to 12 times.

SAFETY TIP As you execute your abdominal contraction, allow your neck to be an extension of your spine. Try to avoid extreme flexion in your neck.

Muscles Involved

Rectus abdominis

Dance Focus

When thinking about using the rectus abdominis, rely not only on the look that this muscle provides you (six-pack abs) but also its responsibilities. You know that this muscle flexes your trunk, so it also can help with added mobility in your stiff thoracic spine. If you are executing a contraction in modern dance, visualize how the rectus abdominis connects your ribs to your pubic bone; maintain that visualization as the muscle creating a concentric contraction to curl your spine. As you extend your spine by performing a cambré back or an arabesque, it engages eccentrically to support and provide a lifting effect for your spine, which will enhance your movements. Using the rectus abdominis effectively will help to increase your core strength and decrease overuse of the hip flexor muscles. Since the abdominals are located in your center, let all of your movement radiate from this point. This is where your body placement finds improvement.

Hip Flexor Isometrics

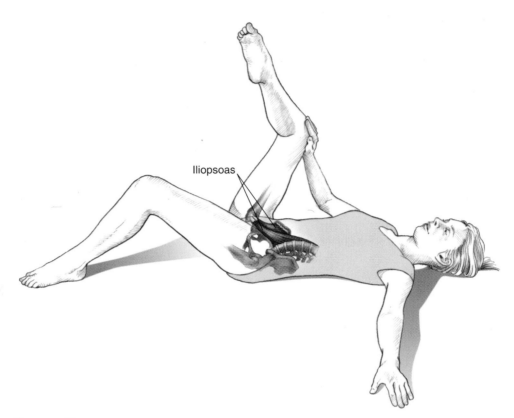

Iliopsoas

Execution

1. Lie on your back with both legs bent and feet on the floor. Coordinate a small pelvic tilt by engaging the lower abdominals and maintain that slight tilt throughout the exercise.

2. Focus on the deep iliopsoas to contract and elevate the thigh toward the same shoulder with slight turnout. Maintain leg height just above 90 degrees.

3. Press against the thigh with one hand to perform an isometric contraction of the iliopsoas. Hold for 4 to 6 counts and then relax. Repeat only 4 times to focus on location of the muscle.

Muscles Involved

Iliopsoas

Dance Focus

This exercise is a simple isometric contraction to help you visualize, locate, and contract the iliopsoas. This is the assistance you need to lift your legs higher than 90 degrees. As this muscle contracts, do not allow the activation of the muscle fibers to pull your lower back into an arched position. Allow the abdominals to contract as well to keep the pelvis from wanting to tip forward. Visualize the muscles that run vertically along the back of your spine, lengthening and stretching as the iliopsoas is contracting. Release the tension in the upper body and send the energy down to the iliopsoas. If you need to, close your eyes and visualize the origin and insertion. Knowing that this muscle connects your lower spine to your femur, imagine pulling your femur closer to your spine, not your spine to your femur. This image will create more awareness of spinal alignment and help to lift your legs higher.

VARIATION

Hip Flexor Neutral

1. Repeat the main exercise. While maintaining the deep iliopsoas contraction, bring your pelvis into a more neutral position. This is challenging! While maintaining control, slowly begin to lengthen the abdominals to slightly roll the pelvis back to neutral. Maintain the contraction of the iliopsoas.

2. On reaching neutral and still feeling the contraction of the iliopsoas, relax and repeat the exercise another 4 times.

⚠️ **SAFETY TIP** Avoid overextending in the lower back as you move into neutral. Move with control.

Spinal Brace

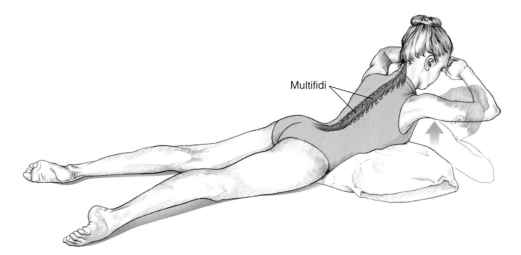

Multifidi

Execution

1. Lie on your front with a small pillow placed under your waist for support and your elbows bent with your hands under your forehead.

2. Inhale to prepare. On exhalation, feel the abdominals tightening and lifting toward your spine; allow the pillow to give you added support. Isometrically contract the small, deep musculature along your spine. Visualize the deep multifidi intertwining along your spine like thick rubber cords. Gently contract along the spine, as if to hover over the pillow.

3. Hold that position as you inhale. With a strong exhalation, continue the deep spinal contraction and slowly move your spine into a slight extension by lifting the upper back. Allow your spine to move into a slight long arch position; emphasize localized, effective movement between each vertebra.

4. The deep spine multifidi muscles contract to support and initiate a small amount of extension along with a cocontraction of the abdominals. This provides significant support and security for your spine. Hold for 4 to 6 counts. On exhalation, slowly return with control. Repeat 10 to 12 times.

⚠️ **SAFETY TIP** Avoid extreme extension in your neck. Maintain abdominal support for stability in the lower back.

Muscles Involved

Multifidi

Dance Focus

Let this small, detailed exercise help you feel the power and strength of the spine to secure your placement. Visualize the small, deep multifidi gently compressing or hugging your spine as if to brace it. Although larger muscles create extension of your spine, use this exercise to emphasize a secure, braced spine. Without the power of the multifidi and coordinating efforts of the abdominals, your spine would collapse under the pressure that dance motions create. This is key to understanding placement and stabilization of the spine before any movements occur with the arms or legs. This will give you excellent placement skills and the needed length for axial elongation. It also distributes the forces evenly. All movement of the arms and legs should be initiated by the contraction of the deep transversus abdominis and the deep multifidi muscles.

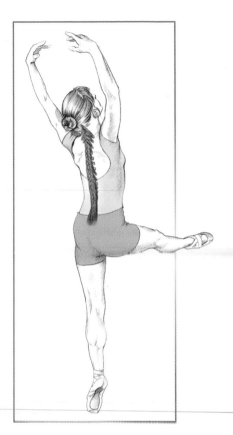

VARIATION

Side Hover

1. Repeat the main exercise. Continue to engage the deep abdominals. Organize your spine to move into a slight lateral (side) bend with inhalation along a lengthening arc.

2. Hold this position for 4 counts. Visualize the deep stabilizing musculature along the spine and the added security of the deep quadratus lumborum connection between the ribs and the pelvis. (You will learn more about the quadratus lumborum muscle in chapter 4.) Return to your starting position; exhale and ease back down. Repeat to the other side and alternate for a total of 4 times on each side.

Ischial Squeeze

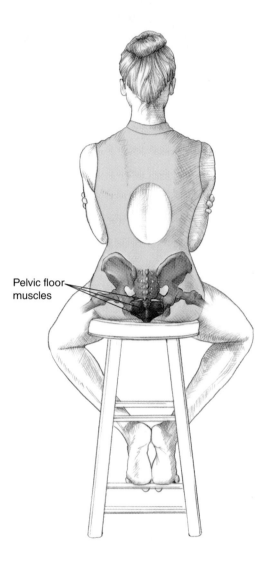

Pelvic floor muscles

Execution

1. Seated on a stool or chair, with legs and hips slightly turned out, rock the pelvis side to side to locate the ischial tuberosities along the lower portion of your pelvis (the sit bones). Return and locate your neutral alignment while seated. Check to make sure you are not in a posterior pelvic tilt or overextending the lower back with an anterior tilt. Rest your crossed arms in front of your body and gently inhale.

2. As you exhale, engage the pelvic floor muscles and pull the sit bones together. Try to organize this muscle contraction with your exhalation. Visualize the muscles of the pelvic floor shortening, allowing the sit bones to pull toward each other. Notice how your spine gently lifts with this supportive contraction.

3. Relax and feel the muscles eccentrically lengthen. Repeat the exercise again; as you begin to experience this contraction, try to visualize the pubic and coccyx bones pulling together as well. Repeat 10 to 12 times.

Muscles Involved

Pelvic floor muscles

Dance Focus

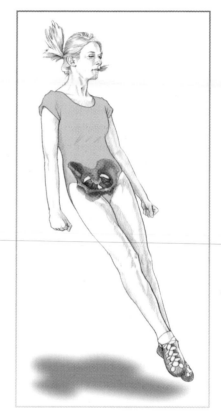

Within all of your creative dance motions, you probably never think about using the pelvic floor muscles. If you notice where the pelvic floor is located, you will understand the significance of its ability to form the basin of support for your pelvis. During technique classes, choreography, and rehearsals, there is hardly ever a mention of these muscles, so take a moment to understand this exercise and its relationship to placement. This is an excellent exercise for emphasizing body awareness; if it doesn't come right away, zero in on the sit bones and visualize the basin shrinking. The movement is very small and fine, but small shifts can lead to large supportive changes. We continue with pelvic floor musculature in chapter 6, but use this exercise as the introduction and become familiar with the lift and support that it provides.

RIBS AND BREATH

Even though breathing is the natural process of bringing oxygen into the lungs, most dancers are unclear about exactly how to breathe! Okay, you know *how* to breathe, but can you use your breath efficiently to reduce tension and improve core strength? How many times do you receive cues to pull your tummy in and up? Typically, you will suck your belly inward, throw your ribs and chest upward, and elevate your shoulders. Now you have increased the tension in the upper body and have actually made it more difficult to breathe! How can you possibly move with ease and grace? Breathing is part of dance and movement. If you're instructing a class, you might want to add breathing exercises into the dance combinations. You could choreograph breathing into the exercises with the music so the dancers become more aware of their breathing patterns. This organized, rhythmic breathing can be a great tool for instilling better breathing habits.

Breath Anatomy

Breathing consists of two phases: inspiration, the period when oxygen flows into the lungs, and expiration, the period when carbon dioxide leaves the lungs. Every part of your body needs oxygen. Oxygen allows cells to release needed energy for the muscular work of dancing. Both phases can be either passive or forced. While reading this book, you are probably unaware of your breathing. At the beginning of your warm-up or technique class, you focus on organizing your body and are unaware of your breathing mechanism. These are examples of quiet, passive breathing. Holding a beautiful balance in relevé would require passive, quiet breathing as well.

The active process of inhalation and exhalation is a more forced act of breathing. This can be described as deeper breathing and uses more musculature for inspiration and expiration. You may find yourself breathing deeper while executing jumping combinations or when the choreography requires more challenging muscle work. Organizing the process of breathing will reduce tension in the upper body, improve oxygen flow to your muscles, and engage your core muscles. All of the exercises in this chapter will help you organize your breathing.

Your lungs are soft, spongy, elastic organs that provide the passageway for air. They are surrounded and structurally supported by your ribs. This chapter is not about overanalyzing every detail of the respiratory muscles, but an overview of this process can assist you in becoming a better dancer. Some of the muscles we focus on first are the diaphragm, the transversus abdominis, and the pelvic floor muscles.

The diaphragm is the most important muscle of the respiratory system. As the primary mover, it is a large, dome-shaped muscle that lies within the rib cage (figure 3.1). It might help to visualize an open parachute inside your rib cage. All of its muscle fibers run up and down, which determine how it contracts. The diaphragm is attached to the lower end of the sternum (chest bone), the lowest six ribs, and the spine. This muscle is responsible for causing the three-dimensional shape changes in the thoracic and abdominal cavity. As you inhale, the diaphragm contracts, moves downward, and flattens out. This contraction allows the lungs and ribs to expand a small amount in all planes, which increases the volume of the thoracic cavity. This expansion moves your ribs in a three-dimensional pattern.

The abdominal wall is made up of four layers; the deepest of the layers is the transversus abdominis muscle, which supports your trunk like a corset. The transversus abdominis muscle fibers run horizontally—the diaphragm weaves into the fibers of the transversus abdominis. On forced exhalation, the transversus abdominis muscle begins to contract, increasing abdominal pressure. Typically, forced exhalation can help you on the downward phase of some movements by enhancing the control of the landing. Try a slow grande battement (high kick); inhale on the preparation and into the leg lift; then actively exhale on the way down. Notice how the exhalation supports the downward phase—you have more control over your leg. The importance of the abdominal wall in supporting the spine and core is discussed in detail in chapter 4. But remember that forced exhalation has a direct relationship with the deep transversus abdominis muscle contracting.

Several layers of muscles support the pelvis, which are also involved in forced exhalation; they connect between the ischium (sit bones), the pubic bone,

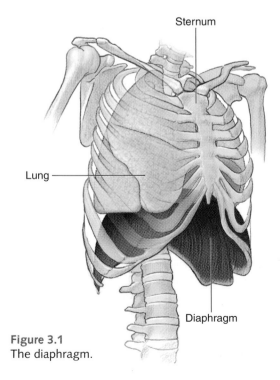

Sternum

Lung

Diaphragm

Figure 3.1
The diaphragm.

and the coccyx (tailbone). These muscles are the pelvic floor muscles. Visualize a diamond shape—the sit bones along the side points of the diamond and the pubic and coccyx bones along the front and back points. During forced exhalation, the muscles that align and attach along the points of the diamond engage, pull together, and provide support for the position of the pelvis. This muscular contraction becomes more apparent while practicing the breathing plié exercise (page 48). Now, when practicing efficient breathing with plié, the upward phase of the plié coordinates the exhalation with engagement of the deep core and the pelvic floor.

Diaphragm Movement

Do you wonder why you are so fatigued after performing certain types of choreography, and do you come to the conclusion that you must keep practicing to build up stamina? How can you build up stamina if you are not getting adequate oxygen? Very simply, on inhalation, the lungs and ribs widen, the diaphragm moves downward, and the abdominal muscles lengthen (it's okay to let your tummy relax a little). On exhalation, the diaphragm moves upward, the ribs return, and the abdominal muscles contract or shorten. There is more emphasis on a three-dimensional movement of the lungs and ribs to provide adequate space for oxygen to enter.

If your stamina is in question, you have probably been rehearsing with upper-chest breathing or shallow breathing while trying to hold your belly in. With upper-chest breathing, air enters only the top of the lungs, which raises your center of gravity. If your chest is too high, you will find it harder to balance and have difficulty with freedom in the shoulders. You have created a leaner look for the moment but have reduced the ability of your diaphragm and lungs to work properly—thus, limiting oxygen intake!

The diaphragm also has muscle attachments to the iliopsoas, which is the powerful hip flexor muscle. By aggressively sucking your tummy in, you also limit the efficient movement of the diaphragm and iliopsoas, which can create unwanted tension in the hip joint. The iliopsoas muscle is composed of two muscles: the iliacus and the psoas major.

- The iliacus originates along the iliac crest and inserts into the femur.
- The psoas major originates along the lumbar vertebrae and the 12th thoracic vertebra and inserts into the femur.

The balance of these two muscles is extremely important for dancers. The iliopsoas connects the spine and pelvis to your legs. A healthy balance between strength and flexibility will help you achieve leg height above 90 degrees and can decrease lower-back pain. When elevating your leg, allow the inhalation to create a lengthening feeling through the spine and the exhalation to create a deep contraction of the abdomen so the hip joint is free to move with ease.

With any forward cambré position, the flexion action deep in the front of the hips compresses the abdomen and brings the diaphragm toward your head, so efficient breathing must occur more in the back of the rib cage. Feel as though you are breathing more into the back of the lower ribs to provide adequate space for taking in oxygen. Tension in the hip joint will cause labored breathing, which limits oxygen flow.

Muscle Action

Other muscles also work during respiration (figure 3.2). The external intercostals lie between the ribs. On inhalation, they contract to open the ribs and bring the sternum forward. Because of the shape of the ribs, they move in a lateral, anterior, and posterior direction to widen the chest. Visualize how a curved bucket handle is raised. The scalene and sternocleidomastoid muscles in the neck, along with the pectoralis major muscle of the chest, can raise the ribs even more. They do have other jobs, but these muscles activate, elevating the ribs during inspiration.

- The scalene muscles originate along the cervical vertebrae and insert into the first two ribs.
- The sternocleidomastoid muscle originates on the sternum and clavicle and inserts into the temporal bone (jaw).
- The pectoralis major originates at the clavicle, sternum, cartilage of ribs 1 to 6, and external oblique and inserts into the humerus bone.

Because these muscles are so involved in inspiration, can you see how over-activating these muscles can create tension in the upper body? When lifting your arms overhead in any dance position, think about elongating axially with the inhalation and widening with the rib cage, not elevating the rib cage. By emphasizing the lateral rib movement, you will create mobility throughout your thoracic spine and freedom in the shoulders.

You have learned that during the active process of forced expiration, the deep abdominal wall contracts along with the pelvic floor. But the intercostal muscles within the ribs, the latissimus dorsi in the back, and the quadratus lumborum also engage to depress the ribs. Get into the habit of using your exhalation to release superficial tension but increase deep abdominal tension. You certainly don't want your audience to see you fighting with tension, panting heavily, and gasping for air. Your audience wants to see incredible skill without physical exhaustion. Think of your diaphragm floating up and down within the movement of the ribs, not creating tension in your jaw, neck, and shoulders. Visualize the lungs moving softly so the ribs can be flexible. When exhaling throughout all of the exercises in this chapter, focus on relaxing the neck and shoulders but increasing the abdominal pressure.

Two other layers of the abdominals are the internal and external oblique muscles. As you will learn in chapter 4, the oblique muscles play a significant role in supporting your trunk and improving basic body placement in dance. The internal oblique muscles have fibrous attachments to the internal intercostals, and the external oblique muscles have fibrous attachments within the external intercostals, again emphasizing the relationship between breathing and the core. Twisting dance movements involve the oblique muscles: The upper body

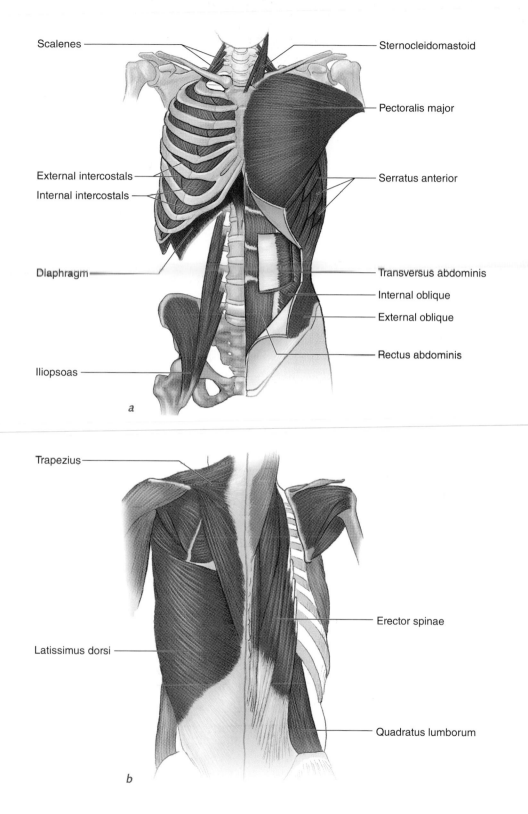

Figure 3.2   Muscles that work during respiration: *(a)* front; *(b)* back.

is rotated in one direction against the resistance of the lower body holding in the opposing direction. To make this twisting of the torso more effective, you must maintain freedom in the shoulders and hips; otherwise it will be too difficult for the diaphragm, abdomen, and ribs to move for breathing. Although it is next to impossible to choreograph breathing into every dance step, practice using the active (forced) exhalation when you need control. Inhale on the preparation and exhale on the movement.

Remember the discussion about the gliding joints? They involve the ribs and their attachments to the spine. There is typically very little movement along the midspine; you want to improve the mobility at these joints to release tension. Use the inhalation to assist you in lengthening through your spine through all planes of movement. The lengthening effect gives you more space between vertebrae and incorporates a small amount of movement along the rib attachments. Let the exhalation phase occur deep within the abdomen and pelvic floor to ground your pelvis and support your spine.

Nasal Breathing

Nasal breathing refers to inhalation and exhalation through the nose. Many yoga exercises emphasize breathing through the nose. Some Pilates exercises are based on inhaling through the nose and exhaling through the mouth. The Alexander technique uses a combination of nasal and mouth breathing, especially in training singers. Inhaling through the nose does help to filter the air, and exhaling through the nose helps to control the amount of carbon dioxide leaving your body. Exhaling through the mouth might help you focus more on deep abdominal contraction. Sometimes when you are short of breath, it might help to exhale through your mouth. It is important for both singers and swimmers to be able to maintain a healthy balance of nasal and mouth breathing. For the purpose of this text, some exercises use both patterns. Excellent breathing techniques can aid in the execution of your dance movements and provide a pleasing quality to your upper body. You can train your lungs and ribs to move more efficiently and limit tension in various joints by practicing the following exercises. Use the exercises in this chapter as part of your daily warm-up as well as part of your cool-down.

Dance-Focused Exercise

Before proceeding to the exercises, take a moment to practice inhaling: Widen through the ribs laterally; on exhalation, feel the ribs returning along with a deep abdominal supportive contraction. Each time you inhale, expand through the ribs and lungs with minimal movement in the upper chest. When you exhale, feel tension leaving the neck and shoulders. Now, practice this breathing style while lying down, seated, and standing just to change your base of support. Try this in front of the mirror and focus on your neck and the top of your shoulders. Are they elevating (meaning you are adding more muscle tension)? You want minimal upper-chest movement and freedom in the neck and shoulders. Look in the mirror to see your ribs moving laterally.

Let your chest feel weightless and your neck be long and free. Try a few arm movements; inhale as the arms go up, and exhale as they return. Think of the smooth movement in the shoulders separate from the widening movement of the lungs and ribs.

Lateral Breathing

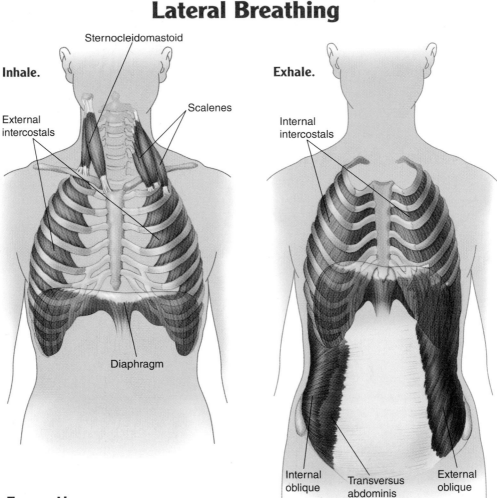

Inhale.

Sternocleidomastoid

Scalenes

External intercostals

Diaphragm

Exhale.

Internal intercostals

Internal oblique

Transversus abdominis

External oblique

Execution

1. Lie faceup with knees bent and feet on the floor and arms at your sides with palms up. Locate your neutral position. On inhalation through the nose, slightly relax the belly, feel the ribs opening and widening, and visualize the diaphragm moving downward. Continue to expand through the middle of the chest and the back of your ribs. Inhale for a slow count of 3; hold on the count of 4. Do not allow your upper chest to lift or your spine to extend.

2. With forced exhalation through the mouth, feel the ribs returning, the midchest relaxing, and the diaphragm elevating. Feel your deep abdominal muscles contracting and remember to release tension in the back of your neck. Feel as though you are gliding your shoulders down toward your hips. Exhale for a count of 4. Repeat the exercise 6 times.

3. You can also try this with one hand on your ribs and one hand on your chest. Focus on lateral rib movement without upper-chest movement; continue to relax the neck, jaw, and throat.

Muscles Involved

Inhalation: Diaphragm, external intercostals, scalenes, sternocleidomastoid

Exhalation: External oblique, internal oblique, transversus abdominis, internal intercostals, latissimus dorsi, quadratus lumborum

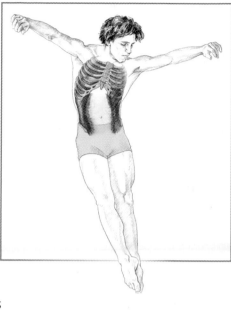

Dance Focus

For visual help with moving the ribs in a more lateral direction, you can try this exercise while sitting or standing in front of a mirror. You can also try this with a partner: Place your hands on the back of your partner's ribs. When your partner inhales, feel the ribs moving into your hands; on your partner's exhalation, gently press into the ribs to assist with the returning of the ribs.

Feel less restriction in your neck and chest; let your spine move because of the antagonistic efforts of the diaphragm and the abdominals. Use your breathing with jumping combinations. Practice small jumps with rhythmic breathing: two small jumps with inhalation and two small jumps with exhalation. You might want to inhale at the top of a larger jump for an added lift and finish with the exhalation for support and control of the landing. Notice how the breathing makes you feel lighter. Remembering your breath and using it effectively will help you move with fluidity and depth.

VARIATION

Lateral Breathing With Resistance

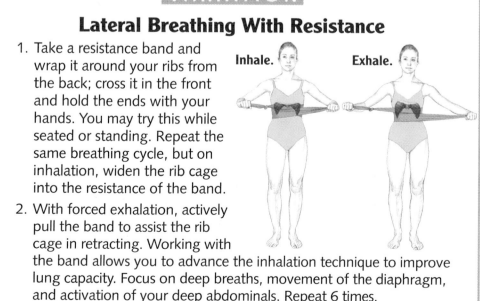

Inhale.

Exhale.

1. Take a resistance band and wrap it around your ribs from the back; cross it in the front and hold the ends with your hands. You may try this while seated or standing. Repeat the same breathing cycle, but on inhalation, widen the rib cage into the resistance of the band.

2. With forced exhalation, actively pull the band to assist the rib cage in retracting. Working with the band allows you to advance the inhalation technique to improve lung capacity. Focus on deep breaths, movement of the diaphragm, and activation of your deep abdominals. Repeat 6 times.

Breathing With Side Bend

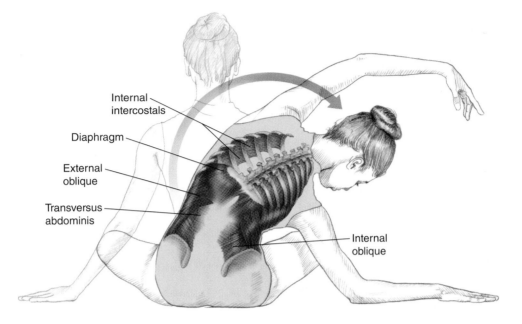

Internal intercostals

Diaphragm

External oblique

Transversus abdominis

Internal oblique

Execution

1. Begin while seated with legs comfortably crossed in front and hands placed by your sides. Locate your neutral position. Inhale through the nose; lengthen through your spine on exhalation through the nose. Engage the core musculature; gently slide the right hand along the floor and bend laterally directly along your frontal plane. Keep both ischium firmly on the floor. Allow your left arm to lift overhead, maintaining width through the chest. Your head may remain facing the front or may be gently turned toward the direction of the bend.

2. Gently rest the right elbow on the floor, continuing to lift through your center. Do not collapse into the elbow. Hold for a breath cycle. Feel the lower ribs of the left rib cage opening wide as you inhale. Be aware of the difference between the left rib cage's expansion and the right's compression.

3. With forced exhalation, feel the left rib cage pulling together and the diaphragm lifting. Engage the deep transversus abdominis and oblique muscles while moving in the longest possible arc. Return back to your seated starting position. Repeat 2 to 4 times each side.

⚠ **SAFETY TIP** Try to avoid letting the neck collapse. Maintain axial length and support.

Muscles Involved

Exhalation: Diaphragm, internal intercostals, transversus abdominis, external oblique, internal oblique

Dance Focus

Allow yourself the privilege of moving smoothly through various planes, trusting the flexibility and stability that your respiratory system provides for you. As you bend your trunk to the side, notice how the top of the lung lifts and the bottom slides downward. Let this principle of internal elasticity give you more fluidity throughout your upper body and more mobility through your thoracic spine. Moving from your center will have more meaning for you when you can feel freedom in your movements. Each time you inhale, allow the air to fill the entire portion of the lungs. As you continue to increase your lung capacity and breathe more comfortably, you will find that you actually have more mobility in your lateral bends. With each exhalation, notice how the abdominals can anchor your pelvis and support your spine. Remember to emphasize moving along the longest arc through the entire range of the side bend.

Breathing With Port de Bras

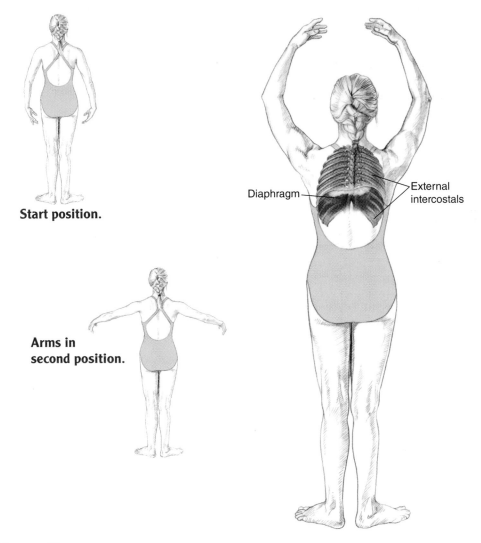

Start position.

Arms in second position.

Diaphragm

External intercostals

Execution

1. Stand comfortably in a wide second position. Focus on neutral align-ment and provide a firm base for your balance. Before beginning, feel the arms lengthening by your sides and a sense of relaxation around your neck and shoulders. Neatly stack your spinal curves on top of each other and feel a gentle lift through your waist.

2. As you begin to inhale through your nose, open your arms to second and continue to lift them to high fifth. Feel the rib cage expanding with air. When the arms are overhead, focus on the weight of the arms moving down the spine to release tension in the neck and shoul-ders.

3. Hold that position briefly and notice how relaxed the back of your neck is. Exhale through your nose as you bring the arms down by your sides, allowing the lungs and ribs to return. Repeat this 4 to 6 times; inhale 4 counts and exhale 8 counts.

⚠ **SAFETY TIP** Avoid overextension in the neck, which compresses the cervical discs; just let your neck be an extension of your spine.

Muscles Involved

Inhalation: Diaphragm, external intercostals

Dance Focus

While this is a very basic breathing exercise, the key is to coordinate the lifting of your arms with effective inspiration. This is what will give your upper body a light, lifted feel without tension surrounding your neck and shoulders. When you breathe in, fill the lungs with oxygen and feel the rib cage expanding and the diaphragm gliding downward—this will allow the lungs to move with ease and flexibility. Visualize the external intercostals contracting to expand your ribs so your upper chest will not elevate. Notice a gentle mobilization where your ribs meet your spine; this will improve your thoracic mobility and spinal alignment. Inhale through your nose and imagine your arms floating up as your ribs swell. Exhale through your mouth when the arms float back down. Repeat this 4 to 6 times. Do not allow your spine to move into extension; this will cause

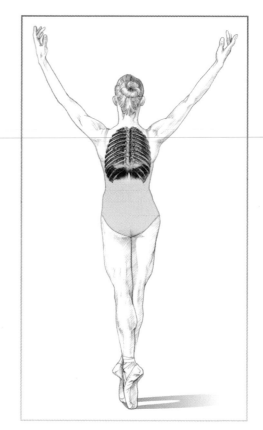

your chest to elevate, your tension to increase, and your alignment to suffer. As breathing and lifting the arms without tension become easier, add relevé and then repeat with jumps and leaps.

Thoracic Extension

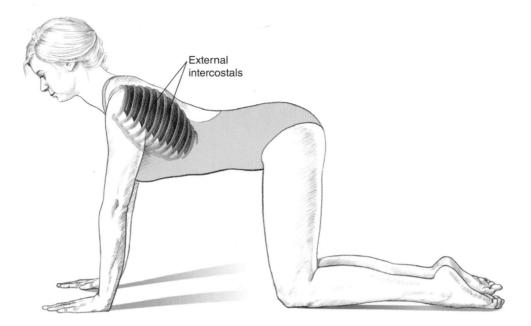

External intercostals

Execution

1. Center yourself comfortably on your hands and knees. Align your shoulders over your wrists and your hips over your knees. Practice several lateral breathing patterns. Remember to release tension in the neck.

2. As you begin to inhale, create an arch through your entire spine. Think about lengthening and moving in a long arc; just allow your head to follow. Don't overextend in the neck. Feel the abdominals being stretched as you expand through the lower ribs. Inhale through the nose for 4 counts.

3. On exhalation through the nose, reverse the arch and move into your starting position. Repeat this 6 times and focus on lengthening through the spine and widening through the ribs. Let all the segments of your spine move equally.

⚠ **SAFETY TIP** **Avoid overextension in the lower segments of the spine.**

Muscles Involved

Inhalation: External intercostals (stretching of abdominal wall)

Dance Focus

Most of the time, inhalation should occur with back-bend positions. But, as you might have noticed, it is difficult to breathe if you are trying to hold your abdominals tight. So, to keep your lower back safe, you must use the entire spine; allow the abdominals to stretch and the chest to expand laterally. Let your inhalation help you extend your spine in that long arch position. Allow the tightness of the abdominals to create pressure against the abdominal cavity; this will give your spine the needed support. Remember to feel your weight into your legs; secure yourself by feeling stable in the lower spine and pelvis. Feel as though you are breathing into the spaces between your ribs, allowing them to expand. You will begin to notice you actually do have more three-dimensional range of motion in your chest.

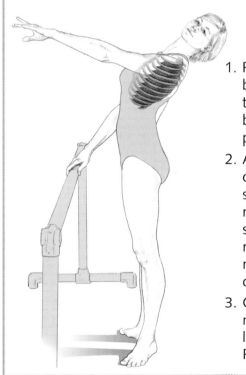

Trunk Extension

1. Repeat this exercise of your upper-back extension in a standing position with one hand on the barre for balance and the other in a high fifth position.

2. As you inhale, widen through your chest. Lengthen and extend the spine, creating a long arch and moving evenly. Do not raise your shoulders and create tension in your neck; continue to feel the abdominals stretching. Your pelvis remains directly over your legs and feet.

3. On exhalation, control the movement on the return and again feel lengthening through the spine. Repeat 4 to 6 times.

Breathing Plié

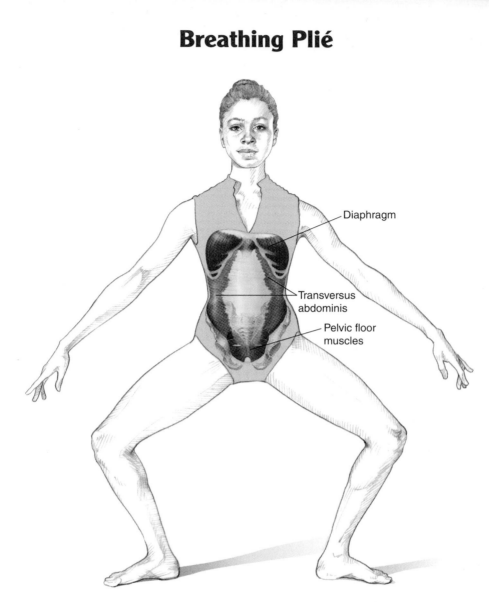

Diaphragm

Transversus abdominis

Pelvic floor muscles

Execution

1. Stand in a firm turned-out second position with arms by your sides. Locate your neutral position. On inhalation through the nose, move into demi-plié while still focusing on axial elongation. Balance your weight evenly throughout your feet. The pelvis remains in a neutral position, and there is an eccentric lengthening of the pelvic floor.

2. With forced exhalation through the mouth, begin the upward phase. As the lungs and ribs return, engage the deep abdominals and feel the pelvic floor contracting. Visualize the ischium pulling together as well as the coccyx and pubic bone pulling together.

3. At the top (completion) of the plié, hold for 3 seconds and focus on neutral spine placement and an isometric contraction of the pelvic floor. Repeat 4 to 6 times. Allow the rhythm of the breathing with the plié to energize your body.

Muscles Involved

Exhalation: Diaphragm, transversus abdominis, pelvic floor muscles

Dance Focus

Plié is so commonly used in all dance styles but may be the most overlooked motion you perform on a daily basis. It prepares you for relevé and for jumps, and it is the transition movement between steps. Without a pliable plié, you are left with choppy, rigid traveling steps. Visualize your three-dimensional movement of the thoracic spine with inhalation as you begin your plié. Maintain axial length along your spine and organize your breath. Allow the inhalation to prepare your body and the exhalation to anchor your lungs, abdominals, and pelvic floor. The upward phase engages the pelvic floor and deep abdomen to give you the firm base to take off for pirouettes, jumping combinations, or relevé en pointe. Try to coordinate the inner thigh muscles' contracting as the legs begin moving together; this contraction will add more support for your pelvis. A firm yet smooth plié with smart breathing will secure your pelvis and lower spine. Your hips will be free to turn in or out without constriction. The quality of all of your movement will improve.

CHAPTER 4

CORE

All movements in dance are generated from your torso, which is your foundation. A firm foundation promotes postural awareness and spinal stability. Your goals are to move through space creating the most challenging and interesting dance steps with ease, right? Achieving these goals requires strong trunk muscles. One of the most basic movements in dance is the plié—whether it is performed parallel, turned in, or turned out, it requires coordination of breath and core strength. When choreography requires your torso to move off balance, the strength of your center keeps your spine from collapsing. Anytime you need to extend your spine while jumping, your core musculature must brace your spine for protection. All aspects of dance can challenge the spine. When you prepare for movement, core activation allows for more control of your movements.

Abdominal training is so popular now, but as a dancer, do you really know how to use the abdominal muscles to help your technique improve? It's not just about performing daily crunches; it's about understanding the anatomy of your center and coordinating the action of the muscles that make up your core. The muscles of the core that contract to stabilize your spine continue to receive a lot of attention with regard to injury prevention and care of the spine. Numerous medical studies prove the connection between the cocontraction of the trunk muscles and a reduction in back injuries. All of these muscles are responsible for excellent posture and a toned waist. It is important for you to strengthen these muscles and apply that strength to your movement, meaning *learn how to dance from your center!*

For spinal support, you need to create this cocontraction of the trunk muscles, which means engaging the transversus abdominis, obliques, pelvic floor, and multifidi. Your core musculature has been described in various ways and has multiple titles: center, trunk, abdomen, midline, powerhouse, spine stabilizers, torso, and abdominal wall. But each title has no significance if you are unable to apply core strength to your dancing.

Core Anatomy

Basic anatomy tells us that the muscles that make up the abdominal wall, beginning with the deepest, are the transversus abdominis, internal and external obliques, and rectus abdominis (figure 4.1). When these muscles contract, they provide security for your spine and spinal curves.

The deep transversus abdominis contains fibers that run horizontally. This layer can be difficult to feel and contract, but it can give you that flat-belly look.

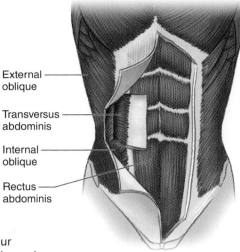

External
oblique

Transversus
abdominis

Internal
oblique

Rectus
abdominis

Figure 4.1   The four
layers of abdominal muscles.

Try to visualize the transversus abdominis muscle as a corset providing a brace effect while you dance.

The internal oblique is a thin layer of muscle located along the side of the trunk. When this muscle contracts, it pulls you into a side bend or rotation on that same side. This action accentuates side cambré movements, twisting motions, and jazzy pelvic isolations. The external oblique muscle is the most superficial and the larger of the two obliques; the fibers run in the opposite direction. When the external oblique muscle is contracted, its primary action is flexing the spine and bending to the side, but it also contracts in spinal rotation from the opposite side. Your oblique muscles help your ribs feel connected to your pelvis. If you feel like you are dancing with your ribs up, think more about the diagonal fibers of the oblique muscles shortening to funnel the ribs in and downward.

The linea alba is a fibrous structure that runs down the center of your abdomen; it separates the right and left rectus abdominis. The superficial rectus abdominis is the long, flat muscle that is actually divided into four sections, giving it that washboard effect. This is an important trunk flexor—again, it is significant in a modern contraction or when rolling up from cambré forward. Remember that the walls of the abdomen have no bony reinforcements, but the layering and directional changes of the fibers combined create great strength.

Basic anatomy also tells us that the deep multifidi muscles run along the posterior aspect of the spine providing spinal support for each vertebra, while the more superficial erector spinae muscles provide support when the spine extends (figure 4.2). The multifidi and the deep transversus abdominis have a higher percentage of type I (slow-twitch) muscle fibers, which makes them so effective for stabilization and posture control. The erector spinae muscles, when tight, contribute to the anterior (forward) tilt of your pelvis. Both multifidi and erector spinae have numerous attachments along the entire spine, some of the ribs, and the sacrum, creating a detailed arrangement of intertwining soft tissue

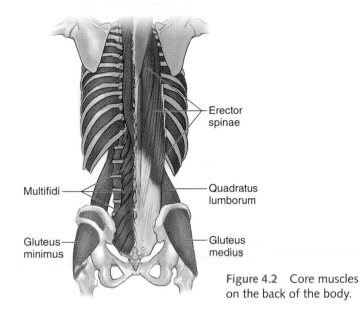

Erector
spinae

Multifidi

Quadratus
lumborum

Gluteus
minimus

Gluteus
medius

Figure 4.2 Core muscles on the back of the body.

structures that provide spinal security. These deep posterior core muscles can provide stability with fine coordination movements as well as larger forceful movements. So, anytime you perform small, fast (petit allegro) footwork or large, sweeping (grande allegro) combinations, there should be an organized contraction of the deep spinal musculature that allows for spinal support. When combined, these muscles primarily make up the core. In figure 4.2, the gluteus medius and minimus have also been included due to their importance in helping to maintain a stable pelvis, which is also important for your placement and dance skills. There is more discussion on this topic in chapter 6.

The muscles lining the deep pelvic region have a significant role in centering, pelvic stability, and postural awareness. Several muscles make up this area, but for this text they are combined and described as the pelvic floor (figure 4.3). The pelvic floor consists of several strong muscles within the bones of the pelvis; visualize a basin as we continue exploring the anatomy of this area. The pelvic bones are made up of two strong hip bones, each consisting of an ilium, ischium, and pubic bone. This basin of bones is enclosed at the front by the pubic symphysis, or joint, and in the back by the sacrum, down to the tailbone (coccyx). While performing various seated floor exercises, notice the two bones that you are sitting on; some jazz dancers call them the booty bones. These two sit bones are at the base of the ischium. Now, you have formed a diamond shape with the bones of the basin—the pubic bone in the front, the sit bones along the sides, and the tailbone in the back. The muscles that line this basin are layered for added strength and can tighten or stretch. Return for a moment to the very first exercise (locating neutral) in chapter 2 (page 20). Extend your lower back and move your pelvis into that forward (anterior) tilted position. Then begin to move your pelvis into your neutral position and visualize the diamond shape shrinking. Continue to practice this, engaging the pelvic floor. Feel the deep security of the lower portion of your trunk.

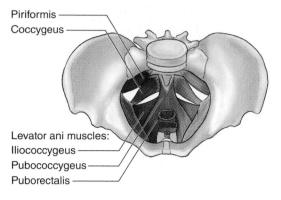

Figure 4.3
Muscles of the pelvic floor.

Fascia can also play a part in awareness of the trunk. Fascia is the superficial tissue lying just under the skin, which anchors the skin to the underlying organs and allows the skin to move freely. Fascia can help protect the deeper body tissues from heat loss and functions as a shock absorber. The thoracolumbar fascia is the membrane of fibers that covers the muscles of the back. It has connections to the core muscles, ribs, vertebrae, and sacrum. Some studies report that the fascia can create tension in coordination with abdominal contraction, which would help to create control for your spine. But if the abdominal muscles are weak and inactive, this tension of the fascia will pull your lower spine into extension, leaving your spine vulnerable to injury. The unsupported extension of the spine along with the tension of the thoracolumbar fascia can create tightness in the lower back.

The iliacus and psoas combine to form the iliopsoas, which connects your spine to your pelvis and femur, also significant in maintaining balance, strength, and flexibility for your center. The iliopsoas originates in the lumbar spine and ilium before inserting into the lesser trochanter of the femur. It works together with the core musculature and the pelvic floor to provide postural control.

Role of the Core in Dance Techniques

Every dance technique requires intense control, which is provided by core strength. Consider the incredible technique of Irish dance. These dancers must hold the spine firm throughout all of their combinations. Their trunk placement must be intensely secure so they can move their legs and feet with incredible speed. In Irish or any other form of dance, the technique is demanding and injury can keep you from training and competing. Include core conditioning into your dance training to improve body placement and reduce risk of injury.

We know that ballroom, social, or partner dance is fluid and beautiful to watch, but it is also quick and powerful. The male partner needs to know where the female dancer's center is at all times. The swing, waltz, and salsa, to name a few, require extreme coordination. Both dancers need to hold their waists firm to provide stability for the pelvis for the quick footwork and challenging partnering movement. Strong core musculature provides for a safe and efficient lift in the upper spine. Once the upper back begins to move safely into extension, a more effective spiral in the spine can be executed. Ballroom encompasses all forms of social dancing: folk, Latin, and vintage dancing. This field is also highly competitive. The contestants are judged not only on footwork and style but on posture, body alignment, and speed. Knowing what we know about deep core strength, wouldn't a series of exercises designed to improve posture and body alignment help to improve the efficiency of the rehears- als? Even the noncompetitive social dancers will benefit from core training to improve their skills. Being centered and maintaining postural control will have long-term positive effects for anyone who enjoys social dancing.

Take a moment to look at the modified swan exercise on page 68. This exercise gives the female partner that beautiful placement of the spine and focuses on gentle thoracic extension. There is an elegant lift in the chest with a long arch through the midback.

Modern choreography requires more tricky and creative jump combinations as well as challenging movement patterns for the spine. Without the ability to compact the core against the spine, the movement will be sloppy and weak. Landing from these nontraditional jumping steps will create injury risks if the spine and pelvis are unprepared. With extreme choreography, dancers must now take their bodies to the extreme and their conditioning to the next level. While some dancers can execute modern contract-and-release styles with ease, other dancers need to practice more with spinal and pelvic stability in mind. Specific exercises in this chapter can help you engage core musculature while putting the spine in more nontraditional lines. Look at the variation to the oblique lift exercise (page 63) as well as the trunk twist (pag 70); both exercises focus on nontraditional movement with muscular support for the spine. The focus is on abdominal bracing while working in various planes and patterns.

Even if you are not interested in a career in professional ballet, you are probably required to take ballet technique classes as part of your training. If you enjoy watching ballet and take a couple of beginner ballet classes each week, you still need control for your spine. While other styles of dance are more grounded, classical ballet gives the illusion of a lifted, light, and airy quality. Ballet is based on various styles—Vaganova, Cechetti, Balanchine, and Bournonville—but the foundation stems from five basic positions with the legs turned out. This alone requires centering and abdominal control. For danc- ers of all ages who perform ballet, a strong center is extremely important for placement, turns, jumps, landing from jumps, and, of course, pointe work. We have Marie Taglioni to thank for being one of the pioneers in creating ballet movement en pointe! Ballet calls for extreme joint motion and torso control. Go back to our plumb line from chapter 2—alignment is crucial for spinal control and injury prevention. Once the alignment is learned, then strengthening can be emphasized.

As with all dance styles, the movement can be divided into phases: prepara- tory, ascending, flight, descending, and landing. The ascending phase usually engages muscles in a concentric-type contraction; the flight phase should have a "lift, hold, and hover" look, requiring extreme core strength and isometric contraction. The descending phase requires an eccentric contraction; some of the muscles lengthen but still support the movement while landing. This eccentric contraction and control on the descending phase are important for reducing injuries. Some studies show that landing from a grande jeté can create a force up to 12 times your body weight. This is why control is the key, and control comes from the core.

Breathing With the Core

Remember that breathing plays a significant role in strengthening the torso. On forcing air out of the lungs, you begin applying intra-abdominal pressure. You need the forced exhalation when you execute a difficult task. Each time you perform some type of a high kick (grande battement), exhale and engage the core. While practicing a turning combination, inhale on the preparation and exhale on the turn; you will feel more security along your spine. While executing a series of small jumping exercises, breathe comfortably but use the rhythm of the combination to keep the balance between the inhalation and the exhalation. The better you get at holding your torso firm, the easier the breathing will be.

While executing the various exercises in this chapter, notice the breathing cues. With each exercise, the deeper you breathe, the more the abdominal muscles work. Remember to inhale through the nose and use the forced exhalation principle to engage the deep stabilizers; this will promote security for your spine. Try exhaling through your nose for most of the exercises, but if you seem to be fatiguing and need to exhale through your mouth, that's fine too.

Dance-Focused Exercise

You can certainly perform the following exercises in the progression given. Be sure to notice the detail of the anatomical drawings and visualize the muscle fiber arrangements; these will help you understand the bracing effect the core has on your spine. Think about where the muscles attach and how that area provides steady support for your placement. You want to build up strength to withstand any force that dance might put on your spine. Contract your core muscles with deep intensity.

This first exercise, described in the sidebar on the following page, is meant to be used as a deep abdominal warm-up while you visualize the bracing effects of your core. The core strengthening exercises continue on the following pages; use this abdominal bracing exercise to prepare for the rest of the series.

Abdominal Bracing

1. Lie on the floor faceup with knees bent and feet comfortably placed on the floor in parallel. Arms can be by your sides.
2. Feel lengthening through your spine, but relax through the base of your neck. Locate your neutral position. Inhale through the nose to prepare while widening through the ribs and lungs.
3. On forced exhalation, begin to contract the deep abdominals as if you were tightening a corset, but maintain neutral position.

Practice this several times and then repeat it while seated and while standing as well. Remember that the spine and pelvis do not move while you learn to isolate your abdominal muscles. This is a basic isometric contraction of the abdominals; the muscles tighten but do not necessarily change shape. Visualize the horizontal fibers tightening as you engage your abdomen (see the illustration on page 52). Remember to tighten the corset without throwing your ribs and chest up. Various terms like *stability, cocontraction,* and *bracing* can be misleading because you might associate those terms with a stiffening feeling along your spine. The word *stiff* is not a word that most of you want to be associated with! But this exercise is quite the opposite. Remember that improving deep core strength will actually enhance controlled movement of your spine. Your jumps will dramatically improve because you have more security along your spine. You will then be able to use the power in your hips and legs to fly.

Side Bend

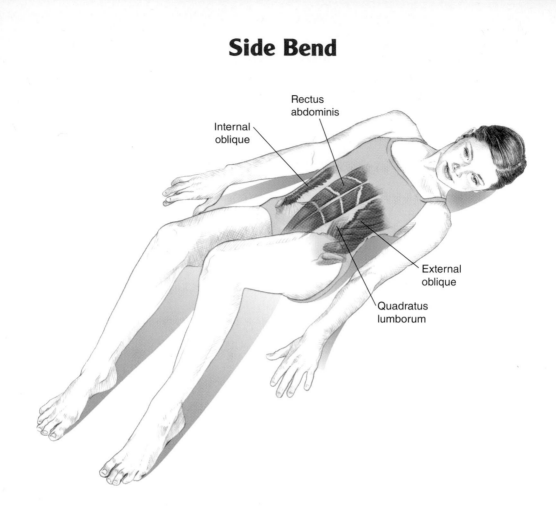

Rectus abdominis

Internal oblique

External oblique

Quadratus lumborum

Execution

1. Lie on the floor with knees bent and feet placed hip-width apart on the floor. Gently rest your arms by your sides. Inhale slowly to prepare.

2. On exhalation, feel axial elongation. Engage your abdominals to raise your trunk slightly. Begin to move into a left side bend, staying along your frontal plane. Your trunk should slightly hover over the floor. Move as far as you can without hiking the right hip; really feel the last rib pulling toward your left hip.

3. Inhale and return to the center with control. Put the same amount of effort into the side bend as you do on the return. Exhale to continue to the other side. Repeat 8 to 10 times each side, working up to 3 sets of 10 repetitions.

SAFETY TIP Move in a long arc to provide more space for the discs. This will avoid compression along your spine and reduce the risk of overuse in any one segment.

Muscles Involved

Rectus abdominis, external oblique, internal oblique, quadratus lumborum

Dance Focus

It's very easy to perform a side bend without effort because gravity will help you to lean over, especially if you are flexible. To perform a secure and aesthetically pleasing cambré side, let the oblique muscles and the quadratus lumborum initiate the movement; actually feel the muscles contracting to pull you into a side bend. This provides the support you need but also prepares you for the next movement, depending on the choreography. Think about lengthening through your spine before you cambré. If you allow gravity to drop you into the side bend, your muscles are not toned; your spinal joints take the stress. It will take more effort to activate your muscles for continuation of the movement, but by then you'll be behind the music! After practicing this exercise, stand and perform a series of side bends first slowly and then quickly. Notice how ready your muscles are. Notice the lift in your trunk, and notice the tone in your waist.

Trunk Curl

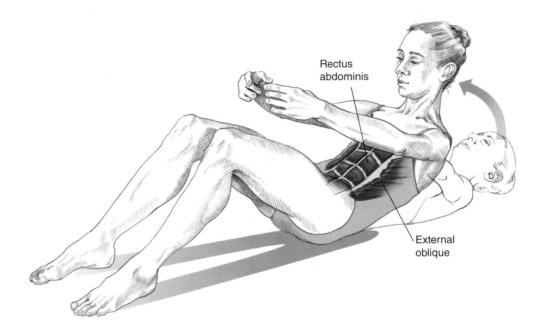

Rectus abdominis

External oblique

Execution

1. Lie on the floor with knees bent and feet placed hip-width apart on the floor. Position your arms in ballet first position. (This can also be done with your arms across your chest, by your sides, or on your shoulders.)

2. On exhalation, contract your rectus abdominis muscle to curl your trunk 45 degrees off the floor. Stabilize your pelvis; your sacrum must stay on the floor. Focus on the upper body moving into flexion; your chin gently comes toward your Adam's apple.

3. Hold this position for 2 or 3 counts and visualize your rectus abdominis muscle fibers shortening. Elevate yourself enough so that your shoulder blades are off the floor. Think about curling throughout your upper spine.

4. Inhale on the controlled return; do not allow gravity to drop you to the floor. Reorganize and repeat 8 to 10 times. Remember to feel the trunk moving toward a stable pelvis. As you get stronger, repeat 6 full sets of 10.

SAFETY TIP Avoid pulling with the neck and overusing the hip flexors. Trying to lift your trunk higher than 45 degrees will activate the deep hip flexors, decreasing the abdominal contraction. Overuse of the hip flexors can cause overextension of the lower spine and is associated with increased risk of lower-back injury. Do not increase your repetitions unless you are able to maintain control and alignment.

Muscles Involved

Rectus abdominis, anterior fibers of the external oblique

Dance Focus

The firm center emphasized in this chapter is not only important for injury prevention, but it is also quite appealing. But remember that you are doing this work to improve your dance technique. Strength in the rectus abdominis can also provide you with more thoracic mobility. The stronger this portion of your trunk is, the more range of motion you will have in your upper body. If you perform choreography that requires you to flex your trunk but maintain a neutral position of the pelvis, you will need to visualize the attachments along the fifth, sixth, and seventh ribs as well as the sternum pulling and shortening vertically to round your spine. If you are required to hold that position and possibly lift a prop or a partner, you will need even more strength and muscle tone. Allow this muscle to provide power for trunk flexion as well as eccentric length for the back of your spine. Don't allow the movement to compress your spine; think more about your spinal muscles lengthening and pushing you along.

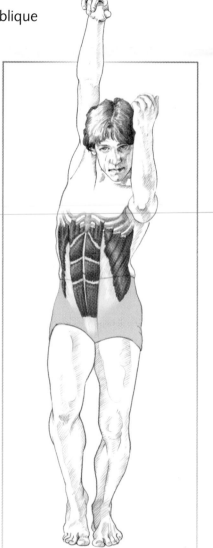

Oblique Lift

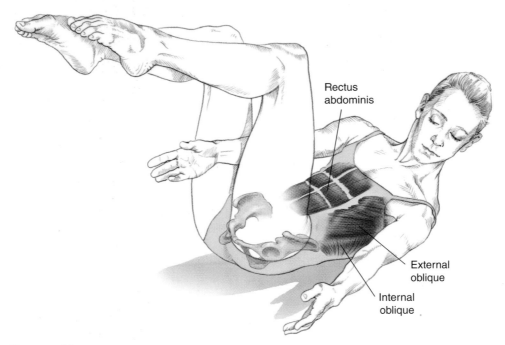

Rectus
abdominis

External
oblique

Internal
oblique

Execution

1. Lie on the floor with your feet raised off the floor so that the knees
   and hips form a 90-degree angle. Place your arms in a basic ballet first
   position. Establish your neutral position and relax the back of your
   neck. Check that your ribs have not opened, causing your upper back
   to extend.

2. As you exhale, curl your trunk as you did in the previous exercise. Add
   rotation to the left, moving your waist along your transverse plane.
   Continue lengthening through the spine, opening through the shoulders and chest. Allow your left arm to move along the outside of your
   left thigh and your right arm to move in between both legs. Focus on
   the oblique muscles elevating and rotating your trunk.

3. Hold that rotation. Reemphasize the pelvis anchoring to the floor. As
   you inhale, slowly return to starting position with control. Repeat on
   the other side. Perform the movement 8 to 10 times on each side;
   work up to 3 sets of 8 to 10 on each side.

⚠ **SAFETY TIP** Avoid twisting the pelvis, which can cause you to
lose stability in the lower segments of the spine. Twisting of the
pelvis lessens the oblique contraction and increases the possibil-
ity of arching or extending the lower spine.

Muscles Involved

Rectus abdominis, external oblique, internal oblique

Dance Focus

All of your turning movements require power through your torso; strength throughout the obliques assists you in accomplishing more refined turns. Modern choreography involves a lot of floor work with lateral and rotational motions; fall-and-rise techniques also need support from the oblique muscles. Jazz warm-ups that focus on isolations will be more effective if the obliques are strong. Each time you perform this exercise, focus on that navel-

to-spine principle; this will give you the added support for the lower segments of your spine as well as a toned waist. Think back to your plumb line posture; the oblique muscle fibers are in an excellent position to assist with proper alignment between the thoracic region and the pelvis. They tend to be overlooked because you give the rectus abdominis so much attention. Balance your exercise program to challenge all of the core muscles.

VARIATION

Advanced Oblique Lift

1. Lie on your left side. Slightly bend the knees and hips. Extend the left arm along the floor overhead. Rest your head on that arm; the right arm lies along your side. Locate your neutral position; do not tuck the pelvis.

2. As you exhale, begin to lift and rotate your trunk. Allow your left arm to sweep along the floor so both arms can reach over the top leg. Your trunk will rotate to the right and flex. Do not let your top hip hike. Maintain that anchored pelvis with knees on the floor.

3. Hold that position for 2 to 4 counts. Focus on the oblique fibers shortening to pull you up. Inhale and slowly return to starting position with control. Repeat 10 to 12 times on each side.

Side Lift

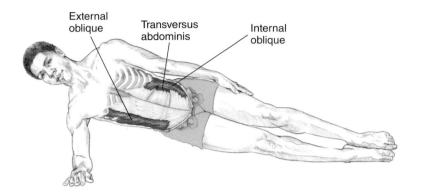

External oblique

Transversus abdominis

Internal oblique

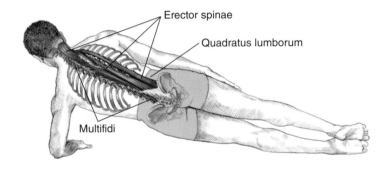

Erector spinae

Quadratus lumborum

Multifidi

Execution

1. Lie on your right side with your legs extended and stacked on top of each other. Your upper body is raised but supported by your right elbow. Allow the right forearm to be placed forward and your left arm rest on your side. Focus on your core; feel your center and your balance. Keep the shoulders down.

2. Inhale to prepare. As you exhale, pull the right shoulder blade down; activate your trunk muscles and elevate your hips. Focus on your center; work within your frontal plane to locate your balance. Maintain this position for 2 to 4 counts.

3. As you inhale, return to the starting position with control. Do not allow gravity to drop you to the floor. Feel your navel pulling in toward your spine for security.

⚠️ **SAFETY TIP** Avoid sinking into the shoulder joint of the supporting arm. Maintain a lifted feeling in your trunk as you press the supporting shoulder blade down.

Muscles Involved

Transversus abdominis, external oblique, internal oblique, quadratus lumborum, erector spinae, multifidi

Dance Focus

This is an excellent exercise for your entire core and really focuses on a firm foundation. You have changed your base of support and need more balance skills to maintain control. Any contemporary style that requires floor work will have a steady and powerful look if you are able to maintain security in your center. As you execute this exercise, visualize the various fiber arrangements within the abdominals all around your spine, and feel them deeply contracting to sustain a secure spine. Visualize your deep multifidi firing to maintain stability along each vertebra. Remember the principle of axial elongation while maintaining an intense contraction of the abdominals. Imagine that you are being lifted by a partner in this pose. You would need to maintain an intense contraction to provide a solid structure for your partner to lift. The timing, coordination, and strength between you and your partner would make it an amazing move.

   When you execute this exercise, other muscles activate, especially the lower trapezius muscles. Those muscles help you maintain stability around your shoulder blades. This is discussed in chapter 5.

Coccyx Balance

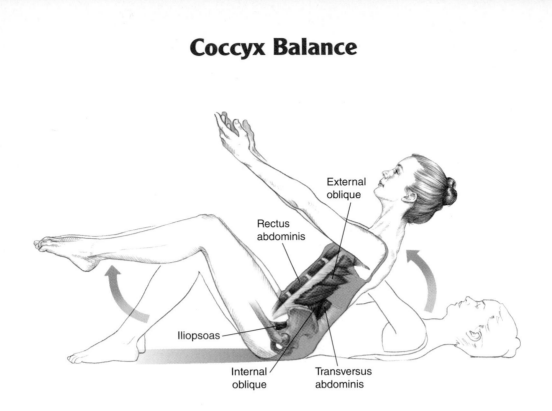

Execution

1. Lie on the floor with knees bent and feet placed hip-width apart on the floor. Place your arms in first position along your sides. Organize your trunk to find your neutral position; inhale to prepare.

2. As you exhale, feel the deep transversus abdominis muscle engage, then allow a small posterior pelvic tilt. Raise the trunk and the knees at the same time while you extend the arms forward.

3. Locate your center; balance the movement with the hip flexor action and the abdominal contraction; feel lower-back stabilization. Inhale as you hold for 4 counts.

4. On exhalation, slowly return to starting position with control. Reemphasize abdominal contraction to protect the lower back. Repeat 8 to 10 times.

⚠ **SAFETY TIP** Perform this exercise only if you have very strong abdominals. If you have weak abdominal muscles, the hip flexors will overpower the movement and pull the lower back into extension.

Muscles Involved

Iliopsoas, transversus abdominis, rectus abdominis, external oblique, internal oblique

Dance Focus

A beautiful balance between abdominal control and hip flexor strength can help you defy gravity. The legs can feel so weighted in an exercise like this that you end up struggling to execute, maintain, and complete the movement. The resistance that the legs provide can pull on your lower spine, putting you at risk for injury; plus, the movement loses aesthetic quality. You want to build a coordinated foundation in your trunk. Dance does not allow you to focus only on one muscle group at a time; it is a collaboration of all muscle groups. You provide the timing of the collaboration. As with all challenging dance patterns, don't let your momentum control the movement. Organize your power because you must return or move into another position with control. Truly understanding the benefits of control will allow you to have the amazing quality of defying gravity.

VARIATION

Advanced Coccyx Balance

1. Beginning in the same starting position, inhale to prepare.
2. On exhalation, engage the deep abdominals. Activate a small posterior pelvic tilt and elevate the trunk and legs together.
3. Allow both knees to extend. Locate your balance and reemphasize the firm center and lower-back control. Inhale for 4 counts.
4. On exhalation, return to the starting position with control. Do not collapse and allow gravity to pull you to the floor.

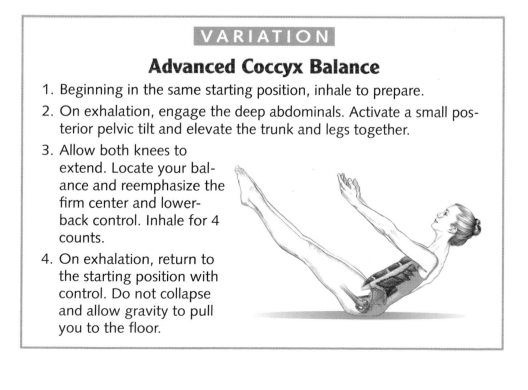

Modified Swan

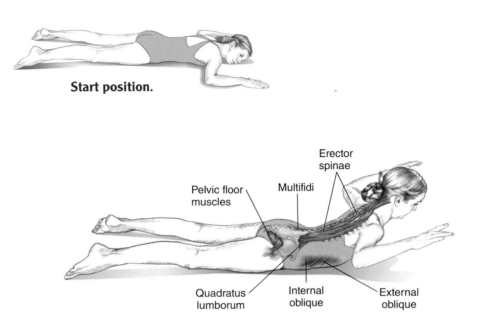

Start position.

Erector spinae

Pelvic floor muscles

Multifidi

Quadratus lumborum

Internal oblique

External oblique

Execution

1. Lie facedown on the floor. Arms rest on the floor with shoulders and elbows at 90 degrees. Legs are extended along the floor, slightly turned out, and just wider than your hips. Lengthen through your spine; gently squeeze the lower buttocks and sit bones.

2. As you inhale, begin to lift your upper body along your sagittal plane while keeping the arms along the frontal plane, maintaining the 90/90 position. Feel extension equally throughout the entire spine. Try to lift the sternum off the floor. Hold for 4 counts.

3. On exhalation, continue the axial elongation and return to starting position with control. Reemphasize abdominal support and contraction of the pelvic floor. Repeat 8 times.

⚠ **SAFETY TIP** Lengthen through the back of the neck to avoid overextending the neck and possibly causing strain. Remember to allow movement to occur along all spinal segments, not just the lower back and neck.

Muscles Involved

Erector spinae, multifidi, pelvic floor muscles, quadratus lumborum, external oblique, internal oblique

Dance Focus

Spinal extension is seen among all dance styles. The Swan Queen shows off her effortless spinal flexibility, as does the advanced jazz dancer with the signature layout. The key is timing and axial elongation. Before you move into any type of spinal extension, remember to elongate through your entire spine; feel as though you are growing taller. Visualize the long, deep multifidi firing for deep control and the erector spinae muscles firing to help you extend your spine. The strength in your abdominals will also brace and support your spine along the front of your body. This is a beautiful preparation for arabesque. Visualize the upper segments of your spine having individual movement in extension and a beautiful lift in your

chest to create this long arch. Always keep in mind that the breathing will help you. Inhale as you extend, feeling the abdomen lengthening and the diaphragm moving down. You will be surprised at how much more range of motion you can attain. Let the exhalation help you on the return by reemphasizing abdominal anchoring and support from the pelvic floor. You are set; your foundation is secure and you are ready to show off your effortless spinal flexibility.

Trunk Twist

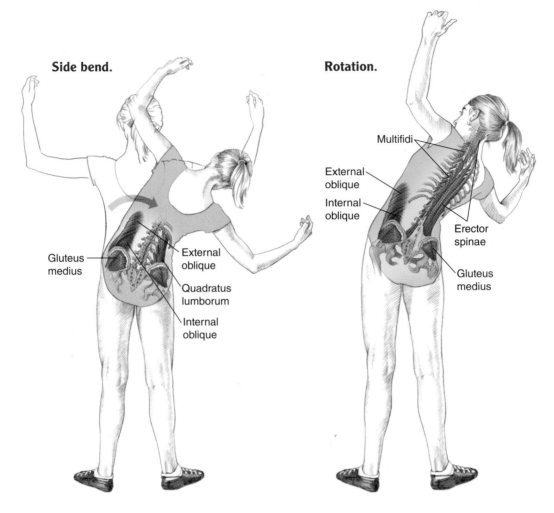

Side bend.

Rotation.

Multifidi

External oblique

Internal oblique

Erector spinae

Gluteus medius

Gluteus medius

External oblique

Quadratus lumborum

Internal oblique

Execution

1. Stand with your legs slightly turned out. Arms and shoulders are in the 90/90 position. Locate your neutral position, creating axial elongation.

2. With inhalation, lift through the center and move into a right side bend along your frontal plane. Visualize movement throughout the entire thoracic spine.

3. Continue into upper-body rotation with extension. Let your waist move along your transverse plane, opening the left shoulder. Allow your head and neck to follow. Maintain width through the chest and shoulders.

4. With control, exhale. Engage the abdominals to reverse the movement and return to starting position. Repeat on the other side for a total of 4 to 6 repetitions on each side.

⚠ SAFETY TIP Reemphasize lower-back support throughout the entire exercise to protect the lower segments of your spine.

Muscles Involved

Side bend: External oblique, internal oblique, quadratus lumborum

Rotation: Multifidi, erector spinae, external oblique, internal oblique

Stability: Gluteus medius

Dance Focus

Let this movement broaden your awareness. Don't just focus on how far you can bend to the side; focus on the articulation through every vertebra in your spine. While moving your trunk sideways to the right, you also have to stabilize your pelvis so your hip doesn't hike on the left side. In jazz warm-ups, you are required to create isolations, separating body sections from others. This exercise promotes that similar skill. In ballet, the grande cambré en rond requires effective movement through your upper back and stabilization through the pelvis. Remember your planes of motion; stay within your frontal plane as you move to the side. So many times you have a tendency to let your lower back arch, open your ribs, and move forward off the

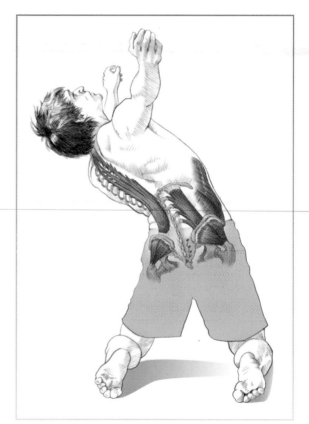

frontal plane. Visualize the four layers of your abdomen and the various directions of the muscle fibers creating your brace. The movement becomes more challenging when your add rotation with extension. Now you are moving along your transverse plane; notice how clean and organized the movement is when you visualize your planes and elongation through the spine and chest. Notice the beautiful curve your spine is creating.

SHOULDER GIRDLE AND ARMS

All forms of dance require efficient arm work for power, aesthetics, balance, and momentum. Your arms are vital for turns and changes in direction. Teachers and choreographers may tell you, "Isolate your arms from your shoulders" and "Keep your shoulders down," but do you really understand those cues? The focus of this chapter is efficiency of movement within the shoulder complex through scapular stability. Once you understand the coordination of arm movement with the upper body, your shoulders will be more secure so your arms, elbows, and wrists can move freely with style and grace.

The shoulder joint is an intricate and very mobile joint, and the muscle control is just as intricate. The elbow and wrist allow for even more detailed movement to create fluidity when you move your arms from one position to the next. Strengthening the muscles that control the shoulder will help you move more from your center. Male dancers need this control for lifting, and female dancers need it for coordinated movements. Even though the majority of injuries that you sustain are lower-extremity injuries, the shoulder should not be forgotten and deserves its own share of the attention.

Bony Anatomy

The bones that make up the shoulder complex are the clavicle (collar bone), scapula (shoulder blade), and humerus (upper arm). The humerus continues down to the elbow joint where it meets the radius and ulna. The radius and ulna continue down to meet the carpal (wrist), metacarpal (hand), and phalanges (fingers). See figure 5.1.

The clavicle bone of the chest forms a joint at the medial portion where it meets the sternum. The outer end of the clavicle meets a small bony protrusion called the acromion process of the scapula. The clavicle bones together create a beautiful line across the front of the sternum and are clearly seen through the skin. This is typically where instructors will guide you to open the front of the chest, the remarkable sensation of presenting yourself to the audience.

The scapula is the triangular-shaped bone that glides along the back of your ribs. It has a shallow socket where the humerus bone inserts; this is called the glenoid cavity. The scapula has an anterior surface (which lies against the ribs) and a posterior surface (which has a slightly elevated portion called the spine). The end of the spine of the scapula becomes the acromion process. There is one other bony protrusion called the coracoid process, which is important for its numerous muscle attachments. The scapula itself is an amazing bone; it has numerous muscle attachments and functions as an anchor for your shoulder.

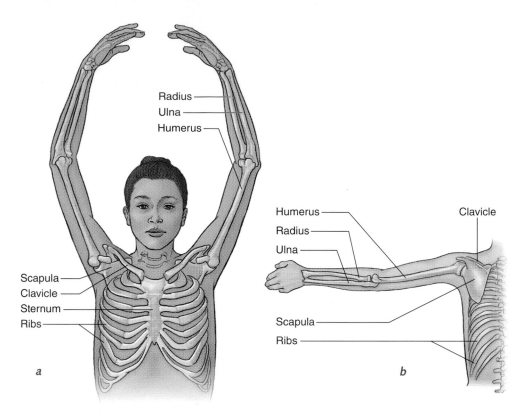

Figure 5.1   Bones of the shoulder complex: *(a)* front; *(b)* back.

Key Joint Motion

Although there are several joints related to the shoulder complex that can create movement, our focus is on two joints in particular: the scapulothoracic joint (where the scapula meets the thoracic spine) and the glenohumeral joint (where the humerus bone meets the glenoid cavity). In its position against the ribs, the scapula can elevate, depress (travel downward), abduct (move away from the center), and adduct (move toward the center). This bone can also curve upward or move in a downward rotational pattern. You have seen winging of the scapula—this is created by the inside corner of the scapula protruding outward, giving the upper back a look of having small wings. Some young, lean female dancers with minor muscular imbalances will display this winging of the scapula. This happens because of muscle weakness and the entire scapula not lying in contact with the rib cage.

The glenoid cavity is a ball-and-socket joint that is held together by strong muscles. This is a relatively strong joint, but it has a shallow cavity—only one-third to one-fourth of the humeral head fits snugly into the cavity. The glenohumeral joint is capable of flexion and extension in the sagittal plane, abduction and adduction in the frontal plane, and internal and external rotation in the transverse plane. This joint can also move in horizontal abduction and adduction. Since the glenohumeral joint is not very deep, stability is important for reducing your risk of injury.

Take a moment to lift your shoulders up and down. Visualize the movement occurring at each scapula and the ribs. Move your arms to your sides and down again along the frontal plane. Visualize the scapular movement as it lies on the ribs. Rotate your humerus bone within the glenoid cavity; note the range of motion at this joint. The muscles that create movement at the glenohumeral joint connect between the humerus and the scapula. The muscles that allow movement to occur around the scapula connect between the scapula and the humerus, sternum, clavicle, spine, and ribs. Strengthening the muscles that attach around the scapula will improve upper-body placement and shoulder alignment and allow the forces of energy and extreme range of motion to be distributed more efficiently through the glenohumeral joint. This will give you better control and help you move more from your center. The basic warm-up that each dance technique requires is not enough for shoulder stability. This is why there are so many shoulder exercises included in this chapter; use them for warm-ups and for strengthening.

The joints between the humerus and the ulna and between the humerus and the radius work together as a hinge joint. A hinge-plus-rotary movement occurs where the lower ends of the radius and ulna meet the carpal bones. This allows for pronation (moving the palm down) or supination (moving the palm up). For some dancers, hyperextension at the elbow (excessive movement past extension) occurs when the arm and forearm are in a straight line. Hyperextension can create stress on the ligaments, especially when falling on an extended elbow. It's important for you to balance the strength between the elbow flexors and extensors to help control the motion at the elbow joint. This principle also comes into play with the numerous bones in the wrist. The scaphoid bone in particular is at risk for injury during a fall and is difficult to see on an X-ray. Balancing flexibility and muscle tone along the forearm provides the beautiful fluidity needed for an elegant port de bras, creative contemporary arm work, strong partnering skills, and gesturing movements.

Muscle Mechanics

The beauty and style of your port de bras come from balanced and powerful shoulder musculature. You know how inspiring it is to create unique designs with your arms, but do you know how to create the designs? Again, understanding which muscles activate will give you a better understanding of that movement. A better understanding means more quality and less quantity of movement.

Rotator Cuff

To understand the mechanics, let's break down the two primary joints that create movement within the shoulder. The glenohumeral joint is stabilized by four deep muscles called the rotator cuff muscles (figure 5.2a). They are the supraspinatus, infraspinatus, teres minor, and subscapularis. Their attachments connect the humeral head with the scapula and allow for stability, some rotational movement, and abduction. The supraspinatus, infraspinatus, and teres minor work together to create an amazing force that keeps the shoulder joint secure so each time you lift your arms, your humerus bone will not pinch against the acromion. If the rotator cuff muscles are weak, the force will be ineffective in creating security for your shoulder joint. This chronic pinching produces pain and swelling and can lead to a condition called impingement syndrome.

Scapula

You have learned that the scapula moves in many planes. When the humerus begins to move, it rises first, followed by the scapula. For example, when lifting your arm into forward flexion, you have approximately 45 to 60 degrees of glenohumeral movement before the scapula begins to move. When lifting your arm to the side, you have about 30 degrees of glenohumeral movement before the scapula moves. The ratio of glenohumeral movement to scapula movement is 2 to 1. Your shoulder blade and upper arm must work together within this ratio to keep the humerus bone from pinching against the acromion. If the muscles that connect to the scapula are weak, the scapula will be ineffective in its job of creating control for your shoulder joint. If you work on strengthening the following muscles, the scapula will have a better chance of being the anchor for your arm movements.

Specific muscles play an essential role in upper-body placement and are responsible for anchoring the scapula and creating efficient movement (figure 5.2a). The trapezius muscle originates at the base of the skull; all cervical and thoracic vertebrae insert on the lateral clavicle, upper acromion, and upper scapular spine. The trapezius is divided into upper, middle, and lower segments. If the upper trapezius is stronger than the other two segments, the shoulders will elevate, creating tension, imbalance, and fatigue. This tension can throw off jumps, turns, and balancing combinations. The lower and middle segments of this muscle are responsible for bringing the shoulder blades down and inward, creating balance. When you need to pull your shoulders down, think about gliding the scapulae down. When you are turning, lifting a partner, holding props, or raising your arms, you can still think about gliding the scapulae down.

The levator scapulae and the rhomboid are muscles located under the trapezius. They originate along various cervical and thoracic vertebrae and insert into the inside edge of the scapula. Because of the attachment location, these muscles can elevate the scapula and create downward rotation. The serratus anterior muscle connects ribs 8 and 9 to the scapula, and the pectoralis minor connects ribs 2 through 5 to the scapula (figure 5.2b). The levator scapulae and rhomboid also provide significant movement for the scapula. The winging scapula is related to weakness of the serratus anterior and lower trapezius muscles.

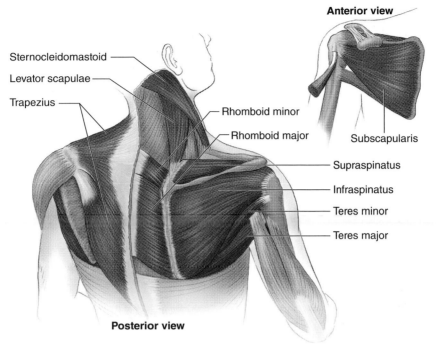

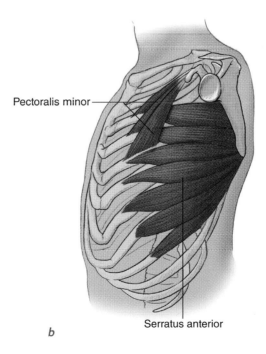

Figure 5.2 *(a)* Muscles of the scapula and rotator cuff. *(b)* Muscles of attachment.

Glenohumeral Muscles

The muscles that connect the humerus bone to the trunk are responsible for the larger dynamic movements of your arms. The pectoralis major is the large muscle in the front of your chest that connects the sternum, clavicle, and various ribs to the humerus bone (figure 5.3a). The pectoralis major can pull your arms forward and together. In almost all turning combinations, the arms will be pulled inward by the pectoralis major. This will generate some of the coordinated power for the turn.

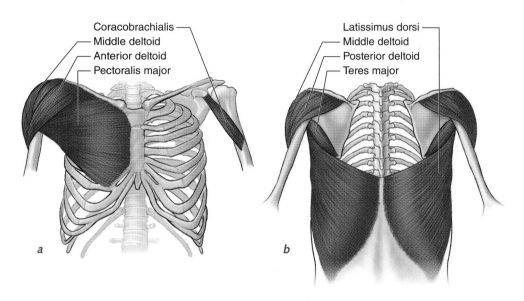

Figure 5.3   Glenohumeral muscles: (a) front; (b) back.

The deltoid muscle divides into three sections: anterior, middle, and posterior. Each prospective section creates movement to the front, side, or back. Hiding under the pectoralis major and anterior deltoid is the coracobrachialis, a small muscle but still capable of producing shoulder flexion and adduction.

The latissimus dorsi is the large muscle of the back that connects the humerus to the last six vertebrae of the thoracic spine, the five lumbar vertebrae, the ilium, the sacrum, and the lower three ribs (figure 5.3b). This muscle creates adduction, internal rotation, extension, and humerus depression. Now you can see how significant each muscle of the shoulder complex is, and you can understand how important it is to balance the strength and flexibility of the muscles that create all of the detailed and elaborate movements that dance choreography will put you through.

Arm Muscles

The elbow joint can flex and extend; it is controlled by specific muscles that create those movements. The biceps brachii flexes the elbow and connects the scapula with the radius bone (figure 5.4a). The triceps extends the elbow

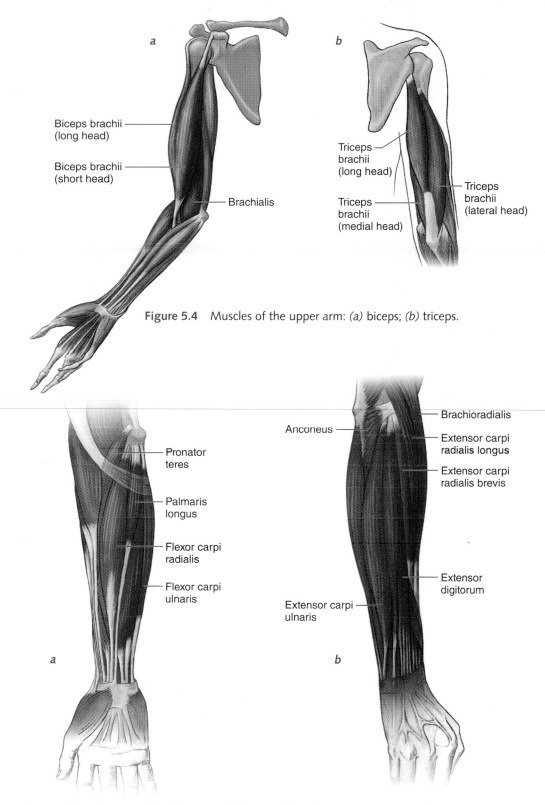

Figure 5.4 Muscles of the upper arm: *(a)* biceps; *(b)* triceps.

Biceps brachii (long head)

Biceps brachii (short head)

Brachialis

Triceps brachii (long head)

Triceps brachii (medial head)

Triceps brachii (lateral head)

Pronator teres

Palmaris longus

Flexor carpi radialis

Flexor carpi ulnaris

Anconeus

Brachioradialis

Extensor carpi radialis longus

Extensor carpi radialis brevis

Extensor digitorum

Extensor carpi ulnaris

a

b

Figure 5.5 Muscles of the forearm: *(a)* flexors; *(b)* extensors.

and the shoulder; it connects the scapula and upper humerus with the ulna bone (figure 5.4*b*). The biceps and triceps both have more than one originating attachment referred to as heads. The biceps has two heads of attachments and the triceps has three heads of attachments. Hiding under the biceps is the brachialis; it connects the lower humerus with the ulna.

The forearm musculature allows for pronation and supination as well as flexion and extension of the wrist (figure 5.5). Strengthening these various small muscles is important for some of the extreme choreography. In some cases, you are asked to stand on your hands, lift other dancers, and fall on your hands. Forearm strength is important for holding props and partnering skills. Many of the various styles of couples dancing require coordinated movements of the hands and the forearms. The exercises in this chapter will stabilize the shoulder, elbow, and wrist.

Carriage of Arms

In classical ballet, carriage of the arms is termed *port de bras,* but in every dance style carriage of the arms completes the movement. All classical ballet port de bras should move with fluidity but must incorporate scapular stability. When the arms move up into a high fifth position, the anterior deltoid and the pectoralis major are the primary movers; the scapula must stabilize and move in an upward rotational pattern, not elevate. The serratus anterior and the lower trapezius must activate to allow the balanced movement of the scapula and humerus. You have a tendency to lift the arms with limited control, allowing the humerus and scapula to elevate and, in turn, overusing the upper trapezius muscles. Remember your 2-to-1 ratio; think about stabilizing the scapula and engaging the lower trapezius and serratus anterior; then allow the humerus to move freely. This strategy is universal for all dance technique and training. The contemporary jazz movements that occur in hip-hop choreography would require the same 2-to-1 principle.

Irish dancers, again, dance primarily with the arms planted neatly at their sides. Their upper bodies must be secure; their scapulae must be anchored to their posterior ribs. Since the elbows are fully extended, the triceps must be strong. To keep the arms securely at their sides, the pectoralis major must hold firm in an isometric contraction. All of the scapular muscles are contracted to stabilize the shoulder blades.

Traditional modern dance takes the arms past their normal range of motion. Your arms will be expected to perform in flexion, extension, internal and external rotation, and variations of all of these positions. Let's examine what happens when you move your arm and shoulder into extension. The posterior deltoid and the latissimus dorsi contract and the scapula needs to rotate downward and adduct slightly; therefore, the rhomboid and lower trapezius need to contract. Now you can see how important it is to strengthen the muscles throughout the upper body.

Dance-Focused Exercise

In most cases, as a dancer, your serratus anterior, rhomboid, and lower trapezius muscles have a tendency to be weak. A lot of exercises in this chapter have additional repetitions to improve your strength. Do not increase the repetitions if you are unable to maintain excellent form. Focus on the alignment of the shoulder joint and ease in the neck and upper shoulders. Use the breathing patterns from chapter 3 to incorporate your core into the exercises. When breathing, remind yourself to move the ribs in a three-dimensional pattern. Once you begin to feel stronger, you will find yourself working more efficiently from your center. Your instructors will also see improvement in how you incorporate corrections from their cueing.

When you receive a cue similar to "Isolate your arms from your shoulders," remember that your scapula has numerous muscular attachments that allow for control so that the humerus, elbow, and wrist can move freely. When you hear "Get your shoulders down," focus less on the upper trapezius and focus more on the lower trapezius, serratus anterior, and rhomboids. If you are struggling with what to do with those winging scapulae, focus on exercising the lower trapezius and the serratus anterior.

External and Internal Rotation

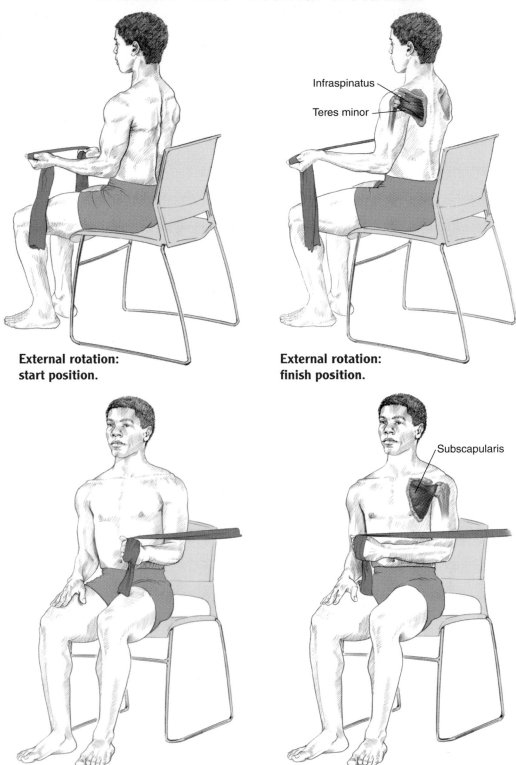

Infraspinatus

Teres minor

Subscapularis

**External rotation:
start position.**

**External rotation:
finish position.**

Internal rotation: start position.

Internal rotation: finish position.

Execution for External Rotation

1. Sit in a chair. Elbows are flexed at 90 degrees and by your sides. Your forearms are forward with palms facing inward. Hold an elastic band taut in both hands. Inhale to prepare, and glide the shoulder blades down.

2. On exhalation, begin to externally rotate your arms against the resistance of the band, keeping your elbows snug against your waist. Hold for 2 to 4 counts and feel the strength within your shoulder joint. Open the front of the chest.

3. As you inhale, slowly return with control, keeping the shoulder blades down. Repeat 12 times, working up to 3 sets of 12.

Execution for Internal Rotation

1. Use the same starting position as for external rotation, but reverse the resistance band, having the resistance coming from the outside. Inhale to prepare, keeping the shoulder blades down.

2. As you exhale, pull inward against the resistance of the band. Hold 2 to 4 counts, maintaining elbows at the waist.

3. Inhale to return with control. Repeat 12 times, working up to 3 sets of 12.

Muscles Involved

External rotation: Teres minor, infraspinatus

Internal rotation: Subscapularis

Dance Focus

Dance classes alone may not provide enough strength for the rotator cuff. Extra conditioning will improve the workings of this joint. While shoulder injuries are not the most common in dance, when they occur you will need treatment, rest, rehabilitation, and improvement in technique, which will put your career on hold. The glenoid humeral joint is already weak because of its shallow cavity. If you are flexible in this joint as some dancers are, then it is even more important to improve joint stability. Loads placed on the shoulder in various styles of dance can be intense; partnering and lifting require strength in all ranges of shoulder motion. You might also be required to fall onto your hands, taking full body weight on the arms. When executing any dance movement where stress is placed through the shoulder, visualize the deep rotator cuff muscles creating a firm brace for protection. This will allow stability in the shoulder joint without sacrificing the fluidity needed through the upper body.

Wall Press

Rhomboid

Scapula

Serratus anterior

Trapezius

Start position.

Finish position.

Execution

1. Stand facing a wall. Lean into the wall with hands wide at shoulder height; elbows remain straight. Reemphasize core control, and inhale to prepare.
2. On exhalation, press against the wall while maintaining straight elbows. Allow both scapulae to move around the rib cage as if the outside edges are trying to pull to the front of your body; the upper back may round slightly.
3. As you inhale, allow the shoulder blades to move back and together. Movement occurs within the scapular region. Repeat 10 to 12 times, working up to 3 sets.

Muscles Involved

Protraction: Serratus anterior

Retraction: Rhomboid, mid- and lower trapezius

Dance Focus

In looking at this movement, you might think that this is important only for male dancers. But actually, weakness in the serratus anterior can cause scapular winging. Weakness in the rhomboid and lower trapezius muscles can cause rounded shoulders; both of these misalignments occur frequently in female dancers as well. If you are an instructor, this information can help you provide important feedback. By visualizing how the scapula works as it moves along the rib cage, you will be able to help your students with exercises to reduce the winging and rounded shoulders. It can be so confusing for dancers to understand corrections on pulling their shoulders down when they are not sure what muscles to use. Focus on sliding the scapulae down and inward as if you wanted to drop them into opposite back pockets. Once you are comfortable with that movement, widen through the chest and visualize the scapulae lying against the ribs. Think about moving only the scapulae forward and back, not the spine, similar to jazz isolations during warm-ups. You are separating the scapulae from your spine. Always let your breathing help you.

VARIATION

Modified Push-Up Plus

1. Begin in a basic push-up position with the knees on the floor. Engage core musculature to create stability along your spine. Wrists should be aligned directly under your shoulders. Glide your scapulae downward toward your hips.

Start position.

2. Inhale to prepare, maintaining trunk stability. On exhalation, feel as though you are pushing the floor away, engaging the serratus anterior and pulling the scapulae into protraction around your rib cage. Keep the elbows softly locked.

3. As you inhale, let the scapulae move back and try to pinch them together, emphasizing shoulder retraction. Maintain trunk stability, and repeat 10 to 12 times.

Finish position.

Port de Bras

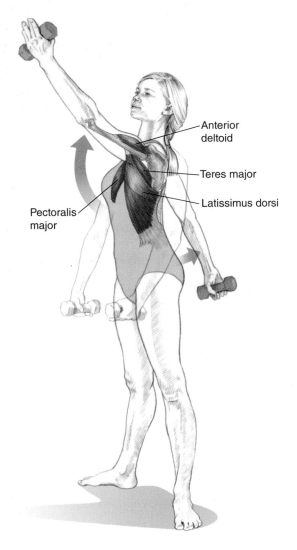

Anterior deltoid

Teres major

Latissimus dorsi

Pectoralis major

Execution

1. Stand firmly with legs hip-width apart, feet either parallel or turned out. Hold small hand weights in both hands. Locate neutral position of spine and pelvis.

2. Move the left arm toward a high fifth position while moving the right arm into shoulder extension. Emphasize scapular stability. Your head and gaze can follow the top arm. Breathe comfortably throughout the movement.

3. Hold for 2 to 4 counts. Feel width through the upper chest. Return with control and repeat on the other side at least 12 times.

SAFETY TIP Organize your placement to maintain a stable spine for safety. While executing arm movements, avoid lifting the chest and extending in the lower back.

Muscles Involved

Shoulder flexion: Anterior deltoid, pectoralis major

Shoulder extension: Pectoralis major, latissimus dorsi, teres major

Dance Focus

Basic ballet emphasizes stylized arm positions isolated from the shoulders. The upper back is secure with a light, lifted effect. The scapula separates from the shoulder joint, emphasizing the stable body placement. As the shoulder moves forward, notice the activation of the anterior deltoid and the pectoralis major, not the upper trapezius, which will cause your shoulder to lift. As the arm moves down from high fifth, gravity provides the majority of the assistance; but as your arm moves behind your body, the shoulder extensors contract. Epaulement provides even more awareness by slightly twisting the trunk to give the carriage of the arms even more dimension. Regardless of the changing movement through the trunk, the arms maintain their elegance by emphasizing scapular

stability. As the arm moves down and to the back, there will be slight internal rotation in the joint. Allow this to occur gently and feel smooth and easy movement in the joint.

Biceps Curl

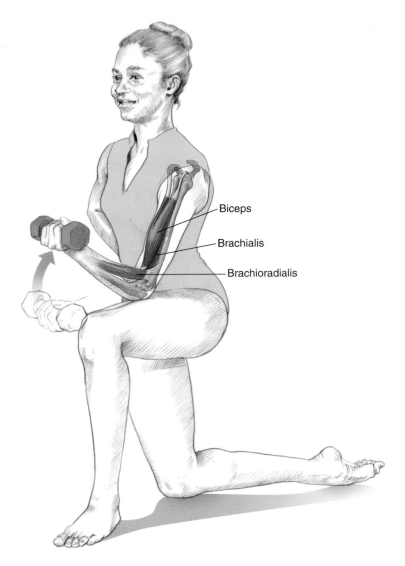

Biceps

Brachialis

Brachioradialis

Execution

1. While kneeling on your right knee, hold a small hand weight in your left hand and rest your elbow on your left thigh. Inhale to prepare.

2. As you exhale, flex the elbow, holding steady in the upper arm. Reemphasize scapular stabilization.

3. Hold for 2 to 4 counts. Focus on the fibers of the biceps shortening, then return slowly with control to starting position. Repeat 10 to 12 times, working up to 3 sets. Start with a light weight and gradually add weight as you get stronger.

Muscles Involved

Biceps brachii, brachialis, brachioradialis

Dance Focus

The action of elbow flexion is used often in various dance movements. Partnering, lifting, falling to the floor, resistance work with another dancer, and pantomime movements require various movements involving elbow flexion. Strength in the biceps protects the elbow from hyperextension injuries but also creates assistance in various shoulder flexion movements. Holding another dancer is challenging, especially when her body weight is completely supported by the anterior muscles of the shoulder and forearm. For the partner carrying the weight, it is extremely important to be able to use the biceps muscles in coordination with shoulder stabilization to reduce risk of injury. Weakness within this muscle will cause faulty alignment and overuse of other structures. For some women who have added

mobility within the elbow joint, muscle strength of the biceps combined with the elbow extensors will create more security for the joint and reduce the risks of injury caused by hyperextension in the elbow.

Triceps Pull

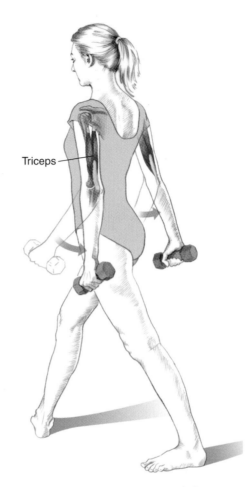

Triceps

Execution

1. Stand with erect posture in a short lunge with legs parallel or turned out. Hold a small hand weight in each hand. Arms are along your sides but slightly extended from the shoulder.

2. Flex the elbows as you inhale. On exhalation, extend the elbows to continue past the body without fully locking the elbow joints. Hold for 2 to 4 counts; feel the strength and contraction of the triceps from the scapulae, through the upper portion of the humerus, and to the back of the elbows.

3. Return to starting position with control. Maintain scapular stabilization. Isolate the humerus during the movement to emphasize shortening of the triceps muscle fibers. Repeat 10 to 12 times, working up to 3 sets. Again, start with light weights and slowly increase the weight.

⚠ **SAFETY TIP** Do not hyperextend the elbow; remember to use the muscles to support the elbow joint. Hyperextension will increase stress on the joint ligaments.

Muscles Involved

Triceps brachii

Dance Focus

The triceps muscle plays a significant role in elbow support; it's involved in shoulder extension and adduction as well. The triceps will help you in the upward phase of push-ups, guiding the elbow into safe extension. Numerous contemporary combinations use the elbow extensors to assist you in raising your body from the floor. The traditional Irish dance posture must incorporate firm elbow extension to maintain security of the elbows with the arms by their sides. Weakness in this area allows the elbow to bend and move during

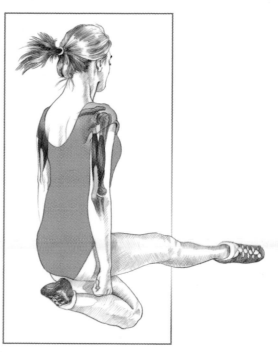

the challenging and quick footwork of that style. Remember to visualize the three attachments (the upper humerus, the scapula, and the elbow) to create stability for the upper arm.

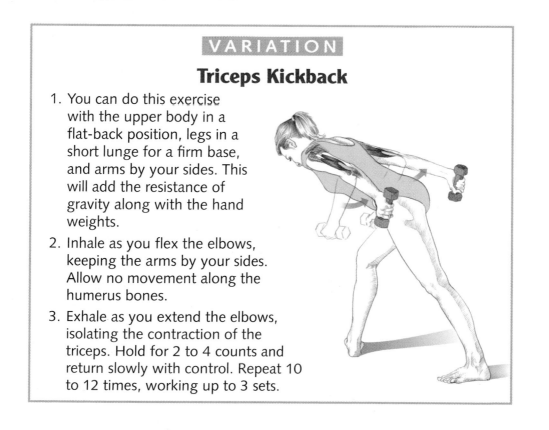

VARIATION

Triceps Kickback

1. You can do this exercise with the upper body in a flat-back position, legs in a short lunge for a firm base, and arms by your sides. This will add the resistance of gravity along with the hand weights.

2. Inhale as you flex the elbows, keeping the arms by your sides. Allow no movement along the humerus bones.

3. Exhale as you extend the elbows, isolating the contraction of the triceps. Hold for 2 to 4 counts and return slowly with control. Repeat 10 to 12 times, working up to 3 sets.

Vs

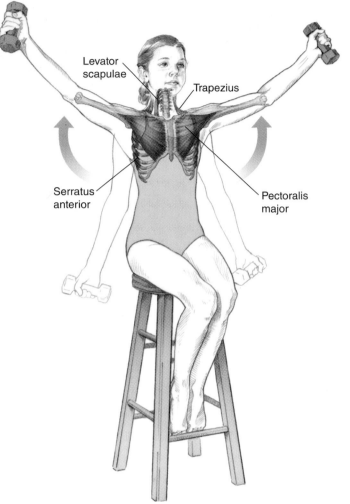

Levator scapulae

Trapezius

Serratus anterior

Pectoralis major

Execution

1. Sit in a chair with erect posture in a neutral position. Arms are by your sides; palms face the front while holding hand weights. The movement will occur along the frontal plane.

2. As you inhale, begin to lift the arms to the sides into a high V position. Emphasize scapular stabilization, widening through the chest. Feel axial elongation through the movement. Remain stable in the pelvis.

3. Hold at the top of the movement for 2 to 4 counts. Reemphasize the scapulae gliding down and inward toward your hips. Return slowly with control on the exhalation. Repeat 10 to 12 times, working up to 3 sets.

Maintain your neutral erect posture. Resist extending or arching through your spine, which means you have lost core control. Practice elevating your arms without lifting through the chest and ribs. Maintain a strong connection with the oblique muscles and the rim of your pelvis as your arms go up. If lifting the arms without spinal extension is too difficult, try it with no weights and exhale as the arms go up. Since inhalation can elevate your chest and facilitate spinal extension, try exhaling as the arms go up.

Muscles Involved

Upward phase: Middle deltoid, supraspinatus, serratus anterior, trapezius

Downward phase: Pectoralis major, rhomboid, levator scapulae

Dance Focus

This is such a beautiful movement, and it is seen in all styles of dance. You can perform this movement with jumps, on relevé, or with a partner—it's always invigorating. Freedom in the shoulder joint gives this arm movement such grace. Focus your energy on the scapulae stabilizing with coordinated upward rotation so the shoulder joints can move with less effort. Maintain placement through your center to show off the ability to isolate the shoulders from the trunk. On the upward phase, feel width through the shoulders without tensing the neck and overusing the upper trapezius. As you begin to bring the arms down, resist gravity and feel the strength through the upper back. Reemphasize deep inhalation on the upward phase and exhalation on the downward phase. Practice without hand weights while jumping as the arms move up—this is where you must control your placement and avoid arching your spine. Let your arms glide upward, keeping you in the air as if you could float over the stage.

Rowing

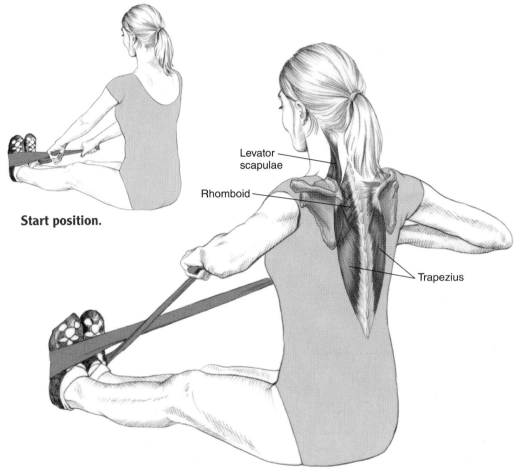

Start position.

Levator scapulae

Rhomboid

Trapezius

Execution

1. While seated on the floor with erect neutral posture, secure a long resistance band around both feet with legs extended out in front. Cross the band and hold it in your hands; elbows are extended with arms in front of you.

2. On inhalation, pull against the resistance of the band with elbows bending at shoulder height and reaching to the back. Feel the scapulae pulling together. Widen through the chest and maintain a firm center.

3. Hold for 2 to 4 counts. Reemphasize scapular adduction, then with exhalation slowly return to starting position. Repeat 10 to 12 times, working up to 3 sets.

⚠️ **SAFETY TIP** Resist spinal extension. As the arms row back, reemphasize core control to maintain a stable spine. Isolate the middle and lower trapezius, not the upper trapezius.

Muscles Involved

Retraction: Trapezius, rhomboid, levator scapulae

Dance Focus

Moving the arms behind the body is common in dance; again, maintenance of scapular control is key to resisting injury. Freedom in the shoulder and stability in the upper body allow for fluidity in all the styles of dance, especially jazz. As the shoulder blades move into retraction, let this open the front of the chest and resist compensation from the trunk. Remember that you are isolating the muscles that create this action, so hold your core firm. Vary the speed of the rowing to simulate varying tempos; this will create more challenge for efficient scapular movement as well as efficient body placement. Your arms will function more effectively when you have a firm and balanced upper body. When you have a strong feeling of awareness in the ability to perform rowing without compensation, increase

the resistance of the band to give you more of a challenge. For a variation, you can repeat this with the elbows pulling back closer to the sides of your body, emphasizing the lower trapezius muscles. This movement through your chest and shoulders really shows off your strength and flexibility. Allow your lungs to truly move in a three-dimensional pattern; you will feel so empowered.

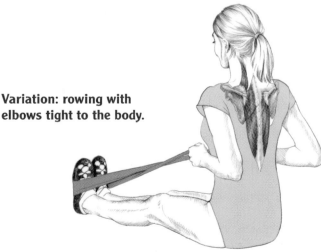

Variation: rowing with elbows tight to the body.

Plank

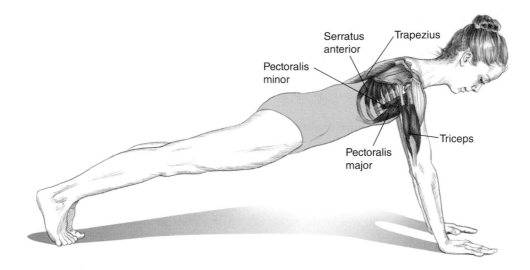

Execution

1. Begin on your hands and knees. Walk your arms out slowly, maintaining control through your center, until your knees fully extend and shoulders align directly over the wrists to plank position. Toes remain in a high relevé position on the floor.

2. Maintain lift in the waist. Feel the scapulae gliding down toward your hips. Lengthen through the spine and keep your head in alignment with the spine.

3. Hold this position, breathing comfortably, for a count of 5. Feel the security in your shoulder joints and the muscles surrounding the scapulae. Slowly walk back to hands and knees with control. Repeat 5 to 10 times.

⚠ **SAFETY TIP** This exercise is advanced and requires firm control in your center. Gravity will pull your lower back toward the floor, causing extension in your spine, which can be harmful. Avoid arching throughout the spine; rest and reorganize if you are unable to maintain safe, secure placement.

Muscles Involved

Shoulder flexion: Anterior deltoid, pectoralis major

Elbow extension: Triceps brachii

Scapular depression: Lower trapezius, pectoralis minor, serratus anterior

Dance Focus

This is a very challenging movement requiring strength throughout the shoulder complex and the core. As you continue to gain strength and flexibility, your physical demands increase as well. Feel the deep stabilizing muscles along your back hugging your spine for support; remember the bracing effect the abdominals provide for stability. Defy the gravity pulling you to the floor; push the floor away with your hands to feel strength through your forearms. The front fall used in some modern techniques requires firm upper-body strength and control as well as core strength. There should be a moment where the body is almost suspended in air, before the hands and arms meet the

floor. Without strength in the shoulder region, the front fall will resemble an unfortunate accident involving an unstable fall! Remind yourself that technique class may not give you the needed strength for the shoulders, so make time to condition your upper body.

Reverse Plank

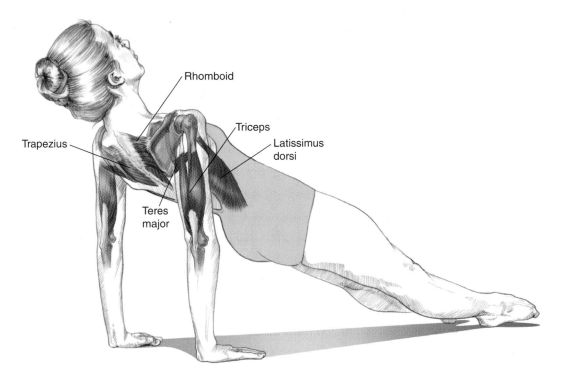

Rhomboid

Triceps

Trapezius

Latissimus dorsi

Teres major

Execution

1. Sit with your legs extended out front. Slightly lean back on your hands, fingers facing forward. Elbows are in a soft but secure position aligned over your wrists. Inhale to prepare.

2. On exhalation, actively pull the scapulae downward and engage your abdominals as you lift your hips to align with the legs. Continue to feel axial elongation and shoulder and scapular stability. Hold for a count of 5.

3. As you inhale, slowly return to the floor, resisting gravity. Maintain control and placement. Repeat 6 to 8 times.

⚠ **SAFETY TIP Do not allow elbow hyperextension or knee hyperextension. Maintain a strong isometric contraction throughout your biceps and triceps to avoid overuse of the small elbow ligaments. Maintain a strong isometric contraction with the hamstrings and quadriceps to avoid overuse of the ligaments in the knee joints.**

Muscles Involved

Elbow extension: Triceps brachii

Shoulder extension: Teres major, latissimus dorsi

Scapular adduction: Middle and lower trapezius, rhomboid

Dance Focus

Creative poses like this are exciting and stimulating for audiences because it's just not your typical dance move! Executing challenging skills where the body weight is bearing down into the wrists and hands can be difficult without significant strength in the upper body to share the load. Think about distributing the forces throughout the entire hand and forearm to resist straining the wrist. Push the floor away with the hands to feel more power in your forearms. As your body begins to elevate, allow the scapulae to move down to provide more upper-body security; this is typically a weak area in many dancers. You might feel a wonderful stretch across the anterior aspect of your shoulder joint; this is the eccentric pull of the biceps, pectoralis major, and anterior rotator cuff. Don't forget to breathe; you may need to focus your breath through the upper rib cage because of the downward pull of the scapulae and the eccentric lengthening of the abdominals.

Dance requires unusual repetitive movement around the hip joint; that movement demands extreme control. Fast and fancy hip movement is the signature for spicy Latin dance. Modern dancers have the strength and agility to work their hips in all planes while shifting weight and still maintaining balance. Tap dancers can move their feet and legs with impeccable speed while the pelvis holds steady. Ballet dancers show off the height of the développé by maintaining strength and flexibility in their hips. All dancers need to understand how the forces of leg movement are distributed through the hip joints and pelvis. Each dance style requires the thigh to work in parallel and internally and externally rotated positions at various times. Understanding how your pelvis works in coordination with your legs can enhance your technique. Your goal is to achieve the desired movement of your legs without losing control of your pelvis.

This chapter focuses on understanding pelvic alignment and femur (thigh) movement. Your pelvis is powerful when organized and balanced. All core musculature inserts into the pelvic region, and most muscles of the thigh originate from the pelvic region—this is quite a powerful intersection! Think about it: Your body's core musculature inserts into the pelvic region, and your leg muscles begin at the pelvis. Your pelvis is the link between your trunk and your legs.

You must learn to move from your center, and your pelvis is the base of your center. It is made up of the ilium, ischium, and pubic bones on each side (figure 6.1). The sacrum is discussed as part of this group as well because it connects the spine with the pelvis. The sacrum is wedged in between the two pelvic bones at the base of the spine. Your center of gravity actually lies just in front of your sacrum. To maintain a balance on one foot, you must maintain your center of gravity in a vertical line that passes through your foot to the floor. Visualize your pelvis and sacrum located over your standing leg for security in balancing.

Along the side of the pelvis is the acetabulum, or deep hip socket. This is the cuplike socket where the head of the femur (thigh bone) inserts. Your femur is the strongest and longest bone in your body. This deep hip socket allows your femur to lift forward, or extend back into arabesque. The acetabulum also allows your thigh to battement to the side as well as turn in or out. The head of the femur angles downward, forming the neck; then it creates two bony prominences: the lesser trochanter and greater trochanter. The lesser trochanter is located medially and the greater trochanter is located laterally. Both of these prominences are important because of the muscles that attach

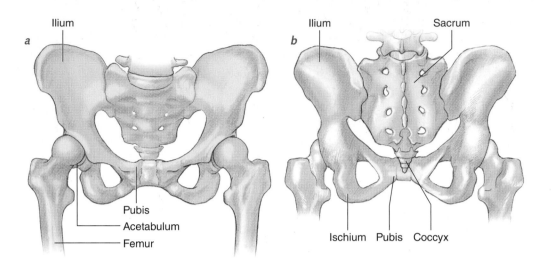

Figure 6.1   Bones of the pelvis: *(a)* front; *(b)* back.

at these points. These muscles help create pelvic stability for your standing leg as well as dance movement for your gesture leg.

Before we continue with alignment and muscles, let's get familiar with the term *hip disassociation.* This term means isolating movement at the hip, separate from the pelvis or spine. Try to tighten the gluteus maximus muscle, and maintain that tightness while you kick your leg to the front. What happens? It's next to impossible to get any height out of the thigh as long as the muscles of your buttocks remain tight! Now, try it again and lengthen the muscles of your buttocks as the leg goes up. So, if you understand the principle of the core musculature inserting into the pelvic region and leg movement starting at the pelvic region, then imagine moving your thighs at the hip joint only. Think about executing a large fan kick; an extremely stable pelvis allows the working leg to relax in the socket to produce fluidity and greater range of motion. The hip joint can better absorb forces that might be harmful to the lower spine.

When you kick (battement) your leg to the front, the anterior muscles contract and the posterior muscles release and lengthen eccentrically. Think back to the discussion of concentric and eccentric muscle work in chapter 1. Concentric contraction describes shortening of the muscle with contraction, and eccentric contraction describes lengthening of the muscle fibers but maintaining strength and muscle tone. When you kick your leg to the front, the gluteus maximus and the erector spinae in your lower back can be trained to lengthen eccentrically while you engage your core to maintain lower-back and pelvic stability. Hip disassociation is the ability to isolate movement at the hip joint independent of your pelvis and spine.

Pelvic Link

You already know that the majority of your injuries occur in the lower extremity. If these injuries are not acute (occurring suddenly), then they are related to faulty technique. Faulty technique usually occurs from poor alignment in the lower spine and pelvis. The iliopsoas muscle is the magic link that connects the lower spine and pelvis with the femur. The psoas connects the lower spine to the femur at the lesser trochanter; the iliacus connects the pelvis to the femur at the lesser trochanter (figure 6.2). Weakness and tightness can result in misalignments of the lower back and pelvis, which then trickle down to the legs. For example, the iliopsoas crosses over the hip joint and can cause snapping as the leg comes down from développé or grande battement. The snapping usually occurs when the iliopsoas tendon moves over the head of the femur or the lesser trochanter; it can produce pain and can develop into an injury that needs to be assessed by a physician. Maintaining strength with turnout throughout the entire range of motion allows the iliopsoas to function in a position that reduces the snapping. Maintaining flexibility can also help keep the tendon from snapping. Typically, the iliopsoas is tight and weak.

The iliopsoas muscle is the major hip flexor; it flexes your hip so you can lift your leg above 90 degrees. Visualize the location of the iliopsoas as it travels from the lower spine to the inside of your upper femur. Imagine the muscle fibers shortening, bringing the femur closer to your trunk. You know that in order to compete, audition, or simply get better as a dancer, you have to get your legs up in the air! There is nothing more frustrating than fighting with your thighs to get your legs up above 90 degrees. (More on that problem in chapter 7.)

Since the iliopsoas originates on the anterior aspect of the lower-spine vertebrae, when it is tight it will pull your lower spine into extension, which tilts the front of the pelvis forward. Even if you understand the concept of trying to hold your pelvis in a neutral position, the movement is next to impossible because your iliopsoas is tight. Dancing in this anterior pelvic tilt and lower-back arch creates inactivity of the abdominals as well as the adductors (inner thigh muscles). This anterior tilt position of the pelvis also causes tightness in the lower-back musculature and creates that shear force against the vertebrae. This book focuses on dance-specific exercises, but the hip flexor stretch in this chapter (page 122) is an important addition. This stretch can be done daily. Try it after your warm-up to encourage effective movement through your hips before you start your center work. Remember your plumb line from chapter 2 and your core work from chapter 4. Reemphasize engaging your core to locate your neutral pelvis position. When you get a correction from an instructor like "Don't arch your lower back," sometimes you will overcompensate and tuck your pelvis under to limit the arch. Tucking the pelvis overworks your gluteus maximus. And you know what happens when you overwork a muscle: It gets bigger! Tucking the pelvis also causes tightness in the hamstrings and unusual pressure on the discs of the lower spine. How can you advance your technique when you are constantly fighting to find your placement? Remember to create length through your spine; locate your neutral pelvis position while engaging the deep core to support the lower back. Abdominal strengthening with iliopsoas and lower-back stretching can help you overcome arching your back. This reorganization of your placement will allow you to move on and advance your skills.

Lateral Hip Power

The gluteus minimus and medius connect the outer surface of the ilium with the lateral area of the greater trochanter (figure 6.2). These two muscles help with abduction and hip stabilization. When you perform parallel side lunges or chassés to the side, the hip abductors are working. The wings that tap dancers execute to the side work the gluteus minimus and medius. Typically, these two muscles are very strong in modern dancers because of the numerous side leg lifts and parallel leg work. Another small muscle called the tensor fasciae latae connects the outer ilium with the iliotibial band. The iliotibial band runs from the ilium down the side of the thigh to the lateral femur, patella, and tibia.

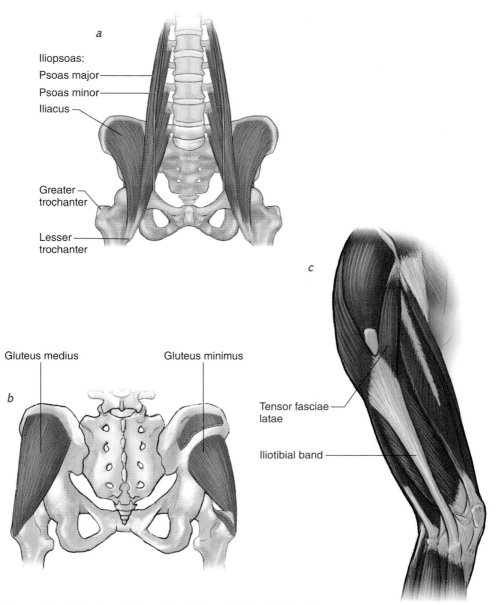

Figure 6.2 Muscles of the pelvis: *(a)* front; *(b)* back; *(c)* side.

This is a very strong band of fascia that in some aspects may work as an external rotator along with the tensor fasciae latae. Nevertheless, a large portion of pelvic stability, which you need for your supporting leg strength, comes from the gluteus medius and minimus. While executing the coupé turn-in and passé press exercises (pages 110 and 112), visualize the location of the hip abductors while focusing on maintaining spinal and pelvic stability.

Control of Pelvic Floor Muscles

The pelvic floor muscles form the bottom of the core and are critical in supporting the pelvis. These muscles are overlooked in dance technique for various reasons. Many instructors are unfamiliar with the function of the pelvic floor muscles, and dancers are uncomfortable discussing this area. You never hear an instructor give cues about the pelvic floor in technique classes!

As discussed in chapter 4, the pelvic floor is a series of muscles that line the base of the pelvis. Remember the pelvic diamond? Visualize the two sit bones, the pubic bone, and the coccyx bone; visualize the muscles that connect the diamond and form a basin. In a basic modern contraction, the pelvis rocks posteriorly, and the sit bones of the pelvic diamond move together very slightly with the contraction of the pelvic floor muscles. On arching the lower back and tilting the pelvis forward, the sit bones move apart, eccentrically lengthening those muscles. There is also a very slight movement of the sacrum, which creates the connection of the diamond from the coccyx to the pubic bone. For example, a demi-plié in second position should start with the pelvis in neutral. On the downward phase, the hips disassociate, the sit bones move away from each other, and the pubic bone and coccyx bones move away from each other. The opposite occurs on the upward phase. In other words, on the downward phase the pelvis stays neutral and the diamond widens; on the upward phase the pelvis continues to stay neutral and the diamond shrinks. Many of the exercises in this chapter focus on strengthening the pelvic floor to improve technique.

Rotation of the Femur

The femur must turn in and out to accommodate all styles of dance. There must be an excellent balance of strength and flexibility between the internal and external rotators. Deep under the gluteus maximus are six small muscles that play a large part in turnout and stabilization of the hip joint. The piriformis muscle connects the sacrum and posterior ilium with the greater trochanter. The obturator internus and obturator externus connect the ischium and pubic bone with the greater trochanter. The gemellus inferior and gemellus superior also connect the lower ischium and sit bones with the greater trochanter. The quadratus femoris also connects the sit bones with the greater trochanter. We'll refer to these turnout muscles as the "deep six."

Internal rotation of the femur is shared by several muscles, some of which are discussed in the next chapter. But let's introduce them now. Two of the hamstring muscles (semitendinosus and semimembranosus) have the ability to internally rotate. The anterior fibers of the gluteus medius and minimus, as well as the tensor fasciae latae, can assist with internal rotation. Remember that the femur can work in various directions without tucking or tilting the pelvis. Excellent hip disassociation skills allow for more effective hip movement and more core stability.

The majority of the turnout must come from movement in the hip socket. Any time you are required to lift your leg while it's turned out, initiate the movement by contracting the deep external hip rotators to fully turn out within the hip socket. Maintain the muscle contraction through the entire movement of the leg while other muscles assist. For example, in arabesque, the deep rotators contract but the gluteus maximus assists as a turnout muscle to help bring the hip into extension. Without the contraction of the deep six rotators, your leg would swing back in parallel! When executing plié, allow the rotators to contract to keep the femurs open along the frontal plane and aligned over the toes. On the downward phase, the inner-thigh muscles assist by working eccentrically; on the upward phase, they work concentrically.

Visualize the location of small external rotators as they connect the femur with the sacrum and lower pelvis. As the muscle fibers contract and shorten, the femur laterally rotates in the socket. The femur can turn out in the hip socket without any unwanted movement in the lower back or pelvis, supporting the hip disassociation theory. Practice moving your femur inward and outward while sitting, lying down, and standing. Focus on movement deep within the socket only; notice how you don't need to twist your pelvis or tuck under to actively rotate your femur in the joint. Just move your thigh, not your pelvis or spine.

Turnout might be physically challenging for you. Familiarity with femoral anteversion will help if you struggle with turnout. *Anteversion* is a term used to describe the angle of the femur; it means turning forward. This placement in the hip socket causes an abnormal internal rotation of the femur, or toeing in, making it anatomically difficult to execute turnout for ballet. This alignment issue causes an anterior tilt of the pelvis. If you try to force more turnout, you will cause twisting of the knees and rolling in at the foot and ankle. This placement might be your personal anatomy and might never allow perfect turnout. If that's the case, then learn to work within your hip's range of motion. Work your feet with less forced turnout and continue to work the turnout muscles properly from the hip. Femoral retroversion is the exact opposite. The angle of the femur allows for more external rotation, or toeing out. This would be more suitable for ballet.

Dance-Focused Exercise

While executing the following exercises, think about maintaining stability in your pelvis and lower spine, and allow the femur to move freely in the hip socket. Even though the legs can be directed into so many amazing moves and angles, you can learn to work the muscles effectively. As one group of muscles work to create the movement, the opposing side must lengthen and the core must secure the movement. It's helpful to inhale on the preparation and exhale on the movement. While working through the exercises, visualize each muscle's location. Focus on the muscle action and how it makes your femur move. To challenge your balance skills, close your eyes for some of the repetitions. Repeat some of the repetitions at a faster pace and notice how changes in tempo challenge your stability. Each exercise directly relates to your technique—use the illustrations to learn which muscles work together.

Plié Heel Squeeze

Quadratus
femoris

Piriformis

Gemellus superior

Obturator
internus

Gemellus inferior

Obturator
externus

Gluteus
maximus

Execution

1. Lie facedown in a slight demi-plié position, with your forehead resting on your hands. Your pelvis must be neutral, not tipped forward with an arch in your lower back. Heels are touching each other. Inhale to prepare.

2. On exhalation, coordinate contraction of the deep abdominals and press the heels together, creating an isometric contraction for the deep rotators and the lower fibers of the gluteus maximus. Hold this position for 6 counts.

3. Relax the contraction as you inhale and prepare to repeat. Push and relax 10 to 12 times.

⚠ **SAFETY TIP** Avoid arching the lower back, which will shorten the deep hip flexors and tighten the lower back. Remain in your natural neutral pelvis with abdominals engaged.

Muscles Involved

Obturator internus, obturator externus, piriformis, quadratus femoris, gemellus inferior, gemellus superior, lower fibers of the gluteus maximus

Dance Focus

One of your goals is to understand the principle of hip disassociation and how it can improve your performance as a dancer in any style of movement. Let this exercise help you to focus on the deep six muscles that externally rotate your legs while resisting the need to tip your pelvis forward or backward. Visualize the femurs working separately from the pelvis. The strength of the contraction and shortening of the deep six should give you the effect of the femurs almost hovering slightly over the floor without strain in the upper thighs or hip flexors. Imagine a grande plié where the thighs are directly to the sides. Also imagine a pas de chat where you are completely turned out along your frontal plane and have a perfectly neutral pelvis.

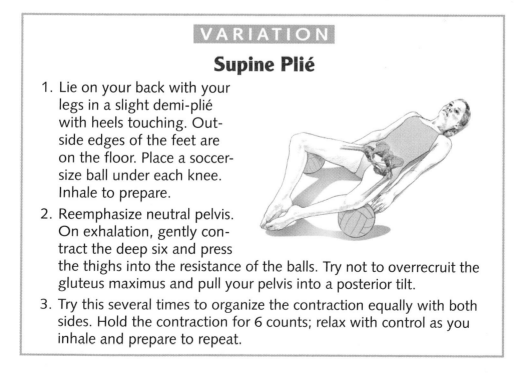

> ## VARIATION
>
> ### Supine Plié
>
> 1. Lie on your back with your legs in a slight demi-plié with heels touching. Outside edges of the feet are on the floor. Place a soccer-size ball under each knee. Inhale to prepare.
>
> 2. Reemphasize neutral pelvis. On exhalation, gently contract the deep six and press the thighs into the resistance of the balls. Try not to overrecruit the gluteus maximus and pull your pelvis into a posterior tilt.
>
> 3. Try this several times to organize the contraction equally with both sides. Hold the contraction for 6 counts; relax with control as you inhale and prepare to repeat.

Coupé Turn-In

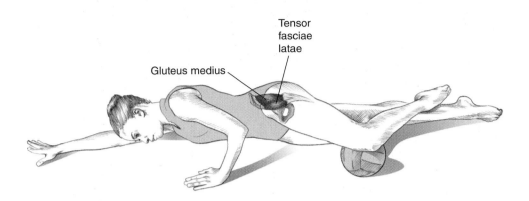

Tensor fasciae latae

Gluteus medius

Execution

1. Begin while lying on your right side. Your bottom arm is extended on the floor overhead; your head rests on the bottom arm. Your top arm is on the floor in front of you. Locate your neutral position. Your top leg is placed in a parallel coupé position; the foot is just above the opposite ankle and the knee is placed on a ball. Organize your trunk and inhale to prepare.

2. On exhalation, reemphasize stability through the core and pelvis. Maintain a strong lift along the waistline on the floor. Gently press the knee into the ball, contracting the internal rotators. Allow the lower leg to move away from the bottom leg, encouraging more turn-in. Hold for 6 counts.

3. As you inhale, slowly return with placement. Repeat 10 to 12 times, working up to 3 sets. Focus on hip disassociation.

⚠ **SAFETY TIP** Anchor your pelvis by reemphasizing core control. Avoid any movement in the lower back. This firm base allows for more fluidity and range of motion in the hip joint and reduces the risk of injury to the lower back. Avoid pelvic tilt; maintain a natural neutral position with the hip flexed.

Muscles Involved

Anterior fibers of the gluteus medius and minimus, tensor fasciae latae

Dance Focus

Strengthening the turn-in muscles is important for maintaining pelvic postural balance. If you have a tendency to walk while your legs are turned out, you may have weakness of the internal rotators; but again, activation must occur without loss of pelvic stability. As you're working in a turned-in position, visualize the front of the thigh turning toward the midsagittal plane and the head of the femur gliding in a slightly posterior direction. You don't have to compensate and move in your lower back. Since the gluteus medius and minimus also provide stabilization for the standing leg, adding turned-in exercises to your fitness program will give you multiple positive results. Hip-hop styles of dance that have developed over the years are exciting to watch and require strength in internal rotation of the hips, as do numerous modern movements.

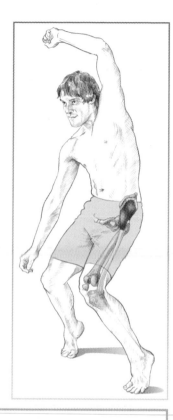

VARIATION

Turn-In With Resistance

1. Lie on your front with the right knee bent and left leg extended along the floor. Place an elastic resistance band around the outside of your right ankle, with the band pulled across to the left side of your body. Steady it by tying it to a table leg or having someone hold it for you. Inhale to prepare.

2. On exhalation, internally rotate the leg against the resistance of the band. Engage the internal rotators while stabilizing the pelvis. Try to move the leg as far as you can while maintaining an anchored pelvis. Hold for 6 counts.

3. As you inhale, return the leg slowly, isolating the internal rotators and separating the movement from the pelvis. Repeat slowly 10 to 12 times. Work up to 3 sets.

Passé Press

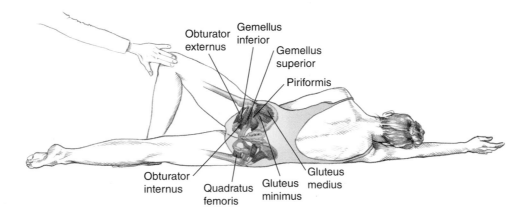

Obturator externus
Gemellus inferior
Gemellus superior
Piriformis
Obturator internus
Quadratus femoris
Gluteus minimus
Gluteus medius

Execution

1. Begin on your right side with the bottom arm overhead and your head resting on it. Your top arm is on the floor in front of you. Place the left leg into passé position and place the foot on the floor in front of the bottom leg. The bottom leg must remain turned out. Feel the outside edge of the left foot against the bottom leg. Reorganize your trunk by engaging your core to feel an added lift along your right side, and inhale to prepare.

2. On exhalation, engage the deep abdominals and begin to contract the deep six rotators, opening the thigh along the frontal plane. Continue the stretch, pressing your leg into the resistance of a partner's hand. Hold for 6 counts and slowly return to prepare to repeat 10 to 12 times.

3. As the deep contraction occurs, feel the separation of your thigh from your pelvis and supporting leg. Keep the turnout working with the bottom leg as well. Resist twisting of the pelvis—you are moving your thigh, not your pelvis.

4. To advance this exercise, repeat in a standing position as in the variation.

⚠ **SAFETY TIP** Maintain trunk stability to support the lower back. Keep the pelvis level to emphasize the deep rotators and hip abductors.

Muscles Involved

Obturator internus, obturator externus, piriformis, quadratus femoris, gemellus inferior, gemellus superior, posterior fibers of the gluteus minimus and medius

Dance Focus

As you perform this exercise, visualize the strength of the passé leg giving you the power to sail in multiple en dehors pirouettes. Turning requires a coordination of force, balance, timing, and strength. Even while performing en dedans pirouettes, you must have an excellent coordinated effort of the working leg turning out in passé and the standing leg turning out. If you lose turnout in one or the other hip, the pirouette comes to an unattractive end. This exercise reinforces the oppositional work between the passé leg turning out and the supporting leg turning out and stabilizing the body.

VARIATION

Resisted Passé

1. From a standing turned-out position while facing the barre, bring the left leg into a passé as in the illustration above. The right leg remains secure and turned out. Reemphasize deep external rotators and deep abdominal muscles for excellent posture.

2. With assistance from a friend as in the illustration on page 112, press your passé leg into the resistance of her hand while firmly maintaining turnout and stability on the standing leg. Hold for 4 counts.

3. Slowly relax and prepare to repeat. Your goal is to execute stability all the way down the chain of the supporting hip and leg as well as isolate the deep six rotators of the passé leg. Repeat 6 times.

⚠️ **SAFETY TIP** Avoid any twisting in the knee of the supporting leg by reemphasizing the stability of the standing leg and the turnout muscles of the standing leg.

Inner-Thigh Press

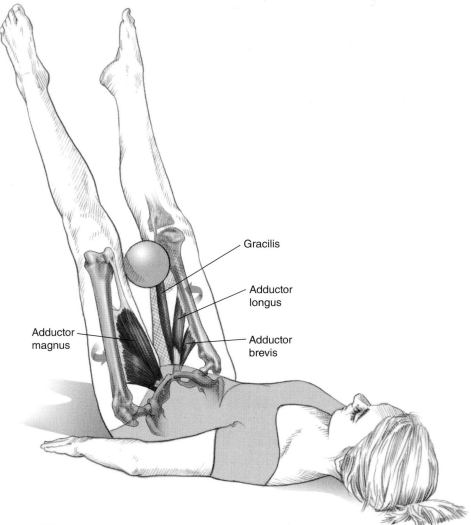

Gracilis

Adductor longus

Adductor magnus

Adductor brevis

Execution

1. While lying on your back with your arms by your sides, lengthen through your spine and organize your trunk to locate your healthy neutral position. Flex the hips to 90 degrees and place a ball between the inner thighs. As you exhale, engage the lower abdominals and extend the knees so that the legs are straight and elevated off the floor, maintaining placement of the ball. Secure a position of leg height that allows your lower spine to remain in neutral.

2. Squeeze the ball within the adductors as you internally rotate and externally rotate. Repeat the hip rotations and ball squeeze for 6 sets.

3. With inhalation, bend the hips and knees to 90 degrees; relax for a moment before you reorganize. Repeat for 4 more sets.

SAFETY TIP Avoid arching the lower back; work to stay in a natural, supported pelvic position by engaging the deep abdominals.

Muscles Involved

Adductor longus, adductor brevis, adductor magnus, gracilis

Dance Focus

Bringing the legs together, crossing positions of the legs, and jumps that have leg beats in the air all require fast and firm adductors. The up phase of the plié requires a concentric contraction of the adductors, and the downward phase requires an eccentric contraction of the adductors. In the lower ranges of leg height, the inner thighs also help with hip flexion and extension. Some of the muscle fibers lie in a position to produce flexion and some lie in a position to produce hip extension. Maintaining a balance between the hip abductors and the hip adductors is another

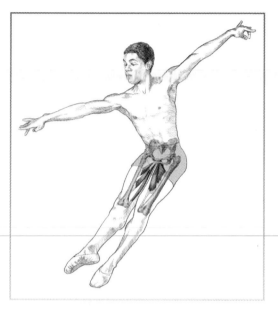

mechanism for pelvic security. You might spend a lot of time stretching the inner thighs for more flexibility, but it is just as important for you to strengthen this area as well.

Arabesque Prep

Tendu derrière position.

90-degree hold.

Semimembranosus

Biceps femoris

Gluteus maximus

Semitendinosus

Execution

1. From a standing position with legs hip-width apart, slowly roll down until the hands are touching the floor (inverted-V position). Reorganize your trunk for balance awareness. Move your right leg into tendu derrière position.

2. As you inhale, move from tendu to arabesque, stopping the movement at 90 degrees. Hold this position for 4 counts as you exhale. On inhalation, continue to lift the leg as high as you can, focusing on the hip extensors.

3. Hold this position for 4 counts as you exhale. Return with control to tendu as you inhale. Resist gravity on the downward phase and focus on eccentric lengthening of the hip extensors. Repeat 3 times parallel and 3 times turned out on each side.

⚠️ **SAFETY TIP** Maintain abdominal support to avoid uncontrollably arching the lower back.

Muscles Involved

Gluteus maximus, biceps femoris, semitendinosus, semimembranosus

Dance Focus

Arabesque can be an amazing movement to watch and execute. It requires detailed coordination of hip extension with spinal extension. In keeping with the principle of hip disassociation, remember to work the thigh against the resistance of uncontrolled lower-back arch and pelvic twisting. Once you have support from your core, hip extensors, and hip rotators, let that power support any pelvic rotation or anterior tilt as the leg goes higher. Feel the movement of arabesque being initiated by the hip extensors along with the eccentric lengthening of the abdominals to protect your spine. Your upper body must tilt forward slightly to cor-

relate with the leg elevating. There is a graceful tug of war going on with the gluteus maximus and hamstrings lifting the thigh and the anterior structures of the core lengthening but maintaining control of your lower back. It is a beautiful example of strength, flexibility, and coordination.

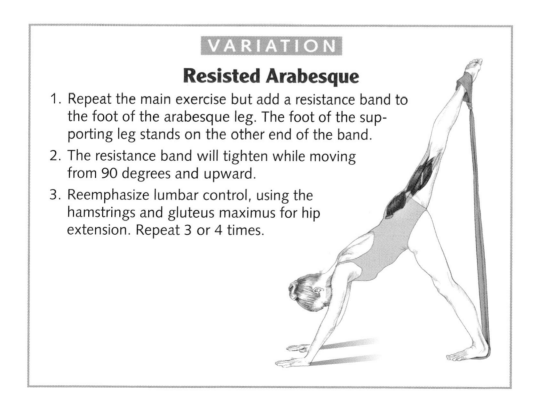

VARIATION

Resisted Arabesque

1. Repeat the main exercise but add a resistance band to the foot of the arabesque leg. The foot of the supporting leg stands on the other end of the band.

2. The resistance band will tighten while moving from 90 degrees and upward.

3. Reemphasize lumbar control, using the hamstrings and gluteus maximus for hip extension. Repeat 3 or 4 times.

Hip Flexor Pulse

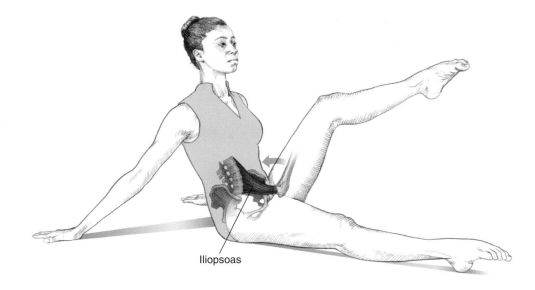

Iliopsoas

Execution

1. Sit on the floor, leaning back slightly on your hands. Your left leg is extended, your right knee is bent, and that foot is on the floor. Visualize the iliopsoas deep under the abdominals, and inhale to prepare.

2. On exhalation, move into a small posterior pelvic tilt and bring the right knee to your chest in parallel. Perform 4 short pulses with the thigh, maintaining a height above 90 degrees. Focus on the iliopsoas fibers shortening to elevate your thigh. Feel both ischial sit bones equally on the floor.

3. Return to starting position with control. Maintain a slight posterior tilt. Repeat for 4 to 6 sets with emphasis on iliopsoas contraction.

⚠ **SAFETY TIP** To emphasize pelvic stability and protect the lower spine, avoid lateral tilt (hip hike) of the working leg.

Muscles Involved

Iliopsoas

Dance Focus

Putting power into the iliopsoas will be your secret to getting those legs up in the air. If you have flexible hamstrings combined with strength and awareness of the iliopsoas, you should be confident that your leg height will improve. The hip flexor pulse exercise is the preparation for a better développé and can be executed with a slight posterior tilt at first; then you can work into a more suitable upright posture for dance. Feel the thigh lifting as high as it can from deep under the low abdominals, and aim the thigh to your ribs. Coordinate the lifting of the right thigh with the dropping of the right ischial sit bone to stay on the floor; this will reduce the tendency of the hip to hike up a bit, which takes the work away from the iliopsoas and places it into the tensor fasciae latae and gluteal muscles. Lifting the thigh demonstrates the concentric contraction, but you can also hold the leg up for an isometric contraction to aid in increased power.

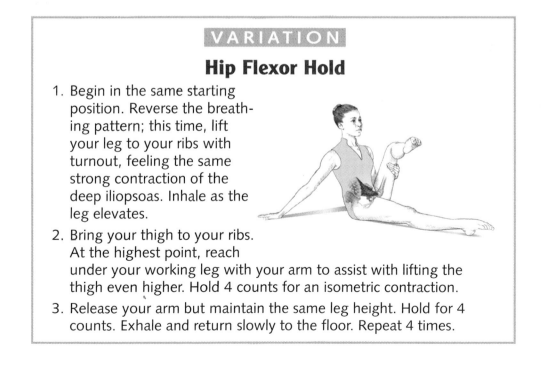

VARIATION

Hip Flexor Hold

1. Begin in the same starting position. Reverse the breathing pattern; this time, lift your leg to your ribs with turnout, feeling the same strong contraction of the deep iliopsoas. Inhale as the leg elevates.

2. Bring your thigh to your ribs. At the highest point, reach under your working leg with your arm to assist with lifting the thigh even higher. Hold 4 counts for an isometric contraction.

3. Release your arm but maintain the same leg height. Hold for 4 counts. Exhale and return slowly to the floor. Repeat 4 times.

Attitude Lift

Turn in.

Iliopsoas

Turn out.

Execution

1. Lie on your left side with the left arm overhead and your head resting on that arm.
Elongate through your spine. Engage the
deep abdominals along both sides of
your body. Your top leg begins the exercise in high attitude à la seconde.

2. Breathing comfortably, begin to
slightly turn the thigh inward for 2
counts but remain in attitude. Turn
the thigh out for 2 counts. Repeat
for 2 sets. Remember to separate
the thigh from the pelvis. Move only the thigh, not the spine or pelvis.

Quadratus femoris

3. While turning the thigh out, elevate your thigh toward your shoulder
by coordinating the contraction of the deep low external rotators with
the power of the iliopsoas. Continue the contraction to increase the
turnout of the thigh as the leg goes higher.

⚠ **SAFETY TIP** Avoid movement of the pelvis; secure the lower spine.

Muscles Involved

Hip flexion: Iliopsoas

External rotation: Quadratus femoris

Dance Focus

If you condition your iliopsoas complex effectively, outside of what any dance technique class might offer, you can increase the height of your legs. While other muscles may be involved in this exercise, take this time to connect the deep iliopsoas and deep low rotators. Notice what happens when you turn your thigh inward—your hip hikes and the muscle contraction moves to the outside of the upper thigh. That is not the place where you want to work your développé! Let the turn-in and turnout aspect of the exercise connect you with the deep low rotators and the deep iliopsoas. Visualize how the iliopsoas complex runs from the lower segments of your spine to the lesser trochanter of your femur. Now, focus on the quadratus femoris muscle as it runs from the outside of the ischial sit bone to the posterior surface of the femur. When one pulls on the femur to lift, the other pulls on the femur to turn it out. It takes coordination, visualization, and action of both to execute an amazing développé to the side.

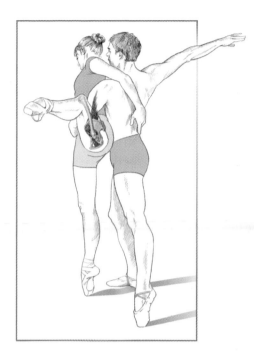

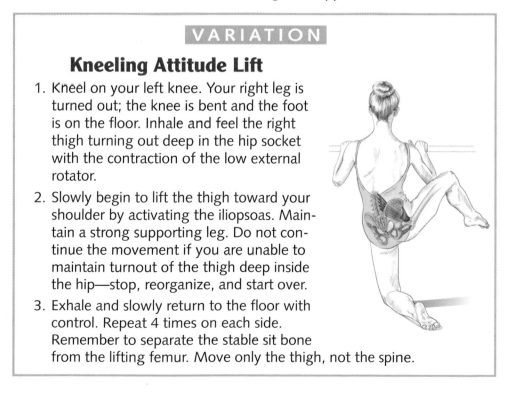

VARIATION

Kneeling Attitude Lift

1. Kneel on your left knee. Your right leg is turned out; the knee is bent and the foot is on the floor. Inhale and feel the right thigh turning out deep in the hip socket with the contraction of the low external rotator.

2. Slowly begin to lift the thigh toward your shoulder by activating the iliopsoas. Maintain a strong supporting leg. Do not continue the movement if you are unable to maintain turnout of the thigh deep inside the hip—stop, reorganize, and start over.

3. Exhale and slowly return to the floor with control. Repeat 4 times on each side. Remember to separate the stable sit bone from the lifting femur. Move only the thigh, not the spine.

Hip Flexor Stretch

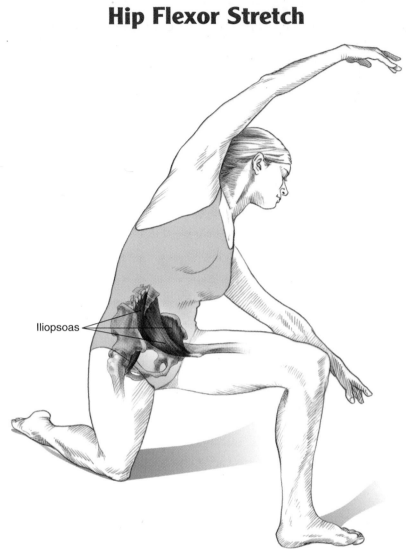

Iliopsoas

Execution

1. Kneel on the right knee. Place your left foot forward on the floor with that knee bent at 90 degrees. Organize your trunk and lengthen through your spine.

2. Create strong posterior pelvic tilt with the abdominals. While lifting through the waist, focus on balance skills. The right leg is in slight hip extension.

3. Begin a long cambré to the left with the right arm overhead. Reemphasize the posterior tilt. Hold the stretch for 45 seconds, taking three long, deep breaths. Feel lengthening through the anterior hip and along the right side of your waist. Slowly return and repeat on each side 3 to 5 times.

Muscles Involved

Iliopsoas

Dance Focus

Working intensely on the deep hip flexors may create unwanted tension. Your goal is to isolate the iliopsoas for lifting the legs above 90 degrees, not to create an overuse syndrome. You might need to repeatedly stretch the hip flexors while you work on strengthening the deep hip flexors. Just remember that you will receive more benefits from your stretches if your body is warmed up. Stretching the front of the hip is also beneficial for working the legs in hip extension. Remain in the posterior tilt for the entire stretch. If your pelvis begins to compensate and tilt forward, you are

losing the effectiveness of the stretch. As the pelvis moves into an anterior tilt, you are actually shortening the hip flexors!

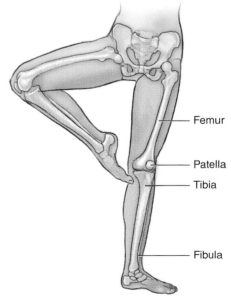

The magic of dance reveals itself in the beauty of the legs and feet. All dance styles show off the capabilities of the legs—they defy gravity and challenge what is humanly possible. This aesthetic quality is how you communicate with your audience. You know you must dance with your entire body, but this chapter looks at the anatomy of your legs and focuses on precision. Precision means the degree of refinement in the movement of your legs. Precise movement requires accuracy and coordinated speed of the contractions of your muscles.

Let's continue by exploring the bones and muscles that contribute to the beauty of your legs. The femur, which is the longest and strongest bone in the body, angles down from the pelvis to form the top of the knee joint (figure 7.1). It has numerous muscle attachments that help to create the precision of your dance movements and skills. The knee joint is a hinge joint supported by strong ligaments. The patella (knee cap) is a free-floating bone within the tendon of the thigh muscle group (quadriceps femoris) inserting into the tibia. During flexion and extension, the patella moves in a gliding pattern but is at risk for injury if there is an imbalance of the quadriceps muscles. Overuse of the outside of the thigh muscles can lead to an abnormal lateral glide of the patella on landing from jumps.

The femur is held tightly into the hip socket, or acetabulum, by strong ligaments: the iliofemoral, pubofemoral, and ischiofemoral ligaments. Notice that their names correlate with the bones they connect. When you lift your legs to the front, all three ligaments relax a bit in order to give you greater range of motion. These ligaments become tight when you lift your legs to the back or tuck your pelvis. The iliofemoral ligament, sometimes called the Y ligament because of its shape, is extremely strong and therefore contributes to hip stability and control of body placement. Tightness in this ligament can limit turnout in your hip. This is why some dancers tilt the pelvis forward, loosening the Y ligament to enable more turnout.

Femur

Patella

Tibia

Fibula

Figure 7.1 Bones of the leg.

There are four ligaments of the knee joint: the medial collateral ligament (which connects the femur and tibia), the lateral collateral ligament (which connects the femur and fibula), the anterior cruciate ligament, and the posterior cruciate ligament (which cross over each other and connect the femur and the tibia). These ligaments provide support and can be severely injured when alignment is compromised, especially when landing from jumps. This relates to precision of movement: The femur needs to mechanically stay aligned over the tibia, especially on landing. Any deviation will allow the femur and tibia to abnormally twist, causing serious stress to the ligaments. The wall sit exercise on page 132 emphasizes lining the knees directly over the toes while moving the legs along the sagittal plane.

Muscle Awareness

In chapter 6 we discussed the lateral hip muscles, the deep external rotators, and the iliopsoas. Now let's look at the anterior (front), medial (side), and other posterior (back) leg muscles. The anterior muscles of the thigh are the quadriceps group. The rectus femoris is the largest muscle of the quadriceps group, and it runs from the iliac spine to the tibia, crossing the hip joint (figure 7.2a). The other three quadriceps muscles are the vastus medialis, vastus intermedius, and vastus lateralis; notice how their names relate to their locations. They originate along the inside, outside, and back of the upper femur and insert into the patellar tendon. All of these muscles flex the hip and extend the knee. We also include the sartorius muscle, which begins at the upper iliac spine and runs down to the inside surface of the tibia. This muscle is the longest in your body, helps to extend the knee, and has a role in turnout. These muscles are very strong and help you keep the knee of the supporting leg straight. They extend the knees on the upward phase of the plié and complete a développé movement.

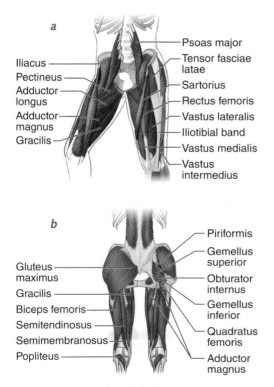

Figure 7.2   Muscles of the leg: (a) front; (b) back.

The adductors, or inner thighs, begin along different aspects of the pubis bone and attach along different aspects of the medial femur. They are the adductor longus, adductor brevis, adductor magnus, pectineus, and gracilis (figure 7.2b). They adduct your thigh and also have the ability to bring your leg to the front and back at lower levels. Many seasoned ballet dancers believe the adductors are important for holding their legs in external rotation, especially when both legs are on the floor. For example, in first position relevé, activating the adductors provides added pelvic stability and security of turnout.

The hamstring muscles line the back of the thigh. The biceps femoris originates along the ischial tuberosity, or sit bone, and femur and inserts into the lateral tibia and fibula. The semitendinosus and semimembranosus originate at the ischial tuberosity and insert into the medial tibia. All of the hamstring muscles flex the knee and extend the hip. The biceps femoris activates strongly in arabesque movements. The hamstrings are also important in body placement. If you activate the hamstring muscles and the abdominals while standing, you can coordinate excellent alignment of the pelvis. This effect will allow the standing leg to be more stable so you don't have to overuse or grip the quadriceps muscles.

We must not forget the gluteus maximus. It originates off the posterior surface of the ilium, sacrum, and coccyx bones and inserts into the femur and also has fibrous attachments along the iliotibial band. Together the gluteus maximus and hamstrings initiate every swing kick to the back, battement derrière, and arabesque. The hamstring curl exercise on page 134 focuses on engaging the deep abdominals while activating the back of the thighs and buttocks. The gluteus maximus is the strongest hip extensor, and some of the lower fibers can play a role in external rotation. But note that if you are unable to locate and use the deep external rotators, you will have a tendency to overuse the gluteus maximus, tuck your pelvis under, and limit turnout.

Precision of Leg Movement

In chapter 6 we discussed the need to improve extensions, but so many dancers struggle with overuse of the quadriceps when attempting to lift the legs higher than 90 degrees. With any leg lifts to the front, especially turned out, the head of the femur must drop downward as the leg begins to elevate (figure 7.3).

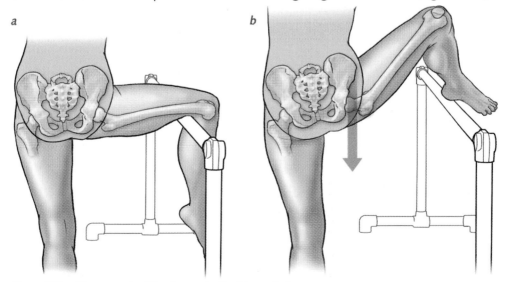

a   b

Figure 7.3 Movement of the femur in the hip socket.

Visualize the sit bone of the leg that's lifting reaching downward toward the floor. The iliopsoas engages to produce a concentric contraction while the gluteus maximus and lower-back muscles lengthen. The supporting leg must hold steady by engaging the hamstrings and hip abductors. Anytime you begin the movement with a hip hike (elevate the hip), you will engage the anterior fibers of the gluteus minimus, gluteus medius, and tensor fasciae latae, which will begin to turn your leg inward. The deep external rotators must work to keep the femur externally rotated throughout the entire range. Don't forget the principle of axial elongation from chapter 2: Lengthen through your spine and engage the core musculature.

If you are performing a développé-type movement, again, the head of the femur must glide downward and continue to turn out. The knee comes into the ribs as high as possible, focusing on the iliopsoas. Then you can begin the concentric contraction of the thighs to straighten the knee. Once you have tightened the quadriceps, they cannot assist you in creating more elevation—your développé is finished. This principle is very similar to the movement of the humeral head of the shoulder complex when lifting the arm.

When your knee is bent, the supporting ligaments loosen, meaning the stability of your knee depends on the strength of the muscles. As the knee extends, a small amount of anatomical rotation occurs within the joint. With this in mind, controlled landings aligning the thighs over the knees and the knees over the toes allow for less chance of knee injury. Anytime the legs are coming downward, either from an aggressive kick or a jump, think about precise control. Your muscles will now need to change course quickly and contract to resist gravity. Returning from grande battement to the front requires reorganization through the trunk but also requires a concentric contraction of the hip extensors. The descending battement exercise on page 142 is a great way to think about control on the return of a movement.

Returning safely and effectively from a jump requires eccentric control through the quadriceps, hamstrings, and lower-leg plantar flexors, which we will get into in the next chapter. Remember from chapter 1 that an eccentric contraction represents the muscles working but lengthening at the same time. Most of the time the downward phase of movement calls for more eccentric contractions for control. Your knee is responsible for approximately one-third of the muscle work on landing. Rolling through the toes and forefoot and into the heels with eccentric control will soften the landing. The knee and hip can then bend with control to absorb the rest of the forces. It is important not to put all of your effort into the takeoff phase and have no control for the landing phase. So many injuries occur while landing from jumps!

Dance-Focused Exercise

Each of the following exercises relates directly to your technique. Think about moving along the most efficient path. In other words, engage your core musculature for supportive placement, and recruit only the muscles needed for accomplishing the movement. Unwanted muscle activity will wear you out; energy conservation allows you to dance longer with precision. For example, you don't need to overwork your neck and shoulders just to lift your leg to the back. Overuse of the neck and shoulders is a hindrance, causes fatigue, and increases injury risks.

Use your new principles of dancing:

1. Plumb line placement for spinal and postural awareness
2. Hip disassociation for thigh movement without spinal or pelvic movement
3. Trunk stabilization to increase controlled movement
4. Effective breathing for engaging core muscles

Of course, it's a lot to think about, but once you practice new movement strategies, it will become automatic. Once it becomes automatic, you will stabilize one body part, move freely with another, and enhance your performance.

Short Arcs

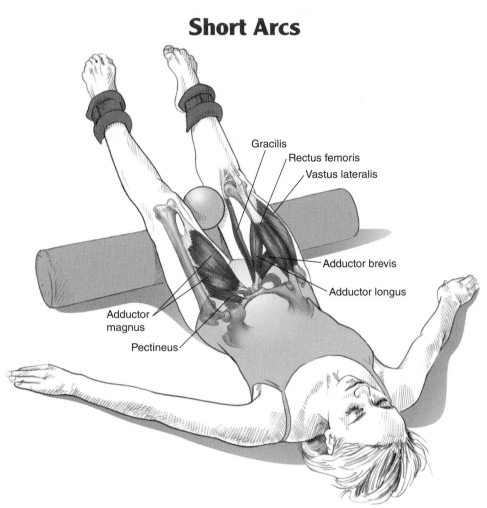

Gracilis
Rectus femoris
Vastus lateralis
Adductor brevis
Adductor longus
Adductor magnus
Pectineus

Execution

1. While lying on your back, place a foam roller or small roll of towels under your knees, a small ball between your knees, and a 3-pound (about 1.5 kg) weight around each ankle. Your feet should be flat on the floor. Recheck your neutral postural alignment. Inhale to begin.

2. As you exhale, coordinate tightening the quadriceps with squeezing the ball to activate the adductors. Extend both knees and hold that position for 2 to 4 counts. Return with control.

3. Focus on lifting the lower legs, not bearing down into the foam roller with the thighs. Repeat 10 to 12 times, then repeat with a quicker knee extension and a slower return 10 to 12 more times. Gradually increase the ankle weights to 5 pounds (about 2.5 kg).

⚠ **SAFETY TIP** To maintain a neutral pelvis, engage the deep transversus abdominis and avoid iliopsoas contraction. Focus on the quadriceps. Avoid knee hyperextension, which increases stress to the posterior knee ligaments.

Muscles Involved

Rectus femoris, vastus medialis, vastus lateralis, adductor longus, adductor brevis, adductor magnus, gracilis, pectineus

Dance Focus

All of the quadriceps are the primary movers for knee extensions, but for this exercise focus on the vastus medialis and the adductors. All of the styles of dance can call for abnormal movement surrounding the knee. It seems the more creative and unusual the choreography, the more attention that movement gets. With that in mind, strengthen the quadriceps together with the adductors to reduce the compressive forces under the patella. Moving the knee between the ranges of 0 to 30 degrees reduces the forces of compression while emphasizing excellent vertical alignment of the patella.

While performing this exercise, think about the lower leg floating up as the thigh contracts or an unfolding of the knee—this visualization will help with completion of développé. The thigh muscles lifting the lower leg is the goal, not pushing downward with the thigh. The Russian pas de chat movement in ballet calls for a strong quadriceps contraction of the leading leg. Whether the pas de chat is large or small, let the thigh muscles lift the tibia.

Focus on the vastus medialis muscle to minimize the tendency of the patella gliding in a lateral direction. Also, vary the tempo of the exercise to simulate jumping: quick on the take-off phase and then slow on the landing phase. The moment the toes reach the floor, the quadriceps must begin to lengthen and remain strong and toned. Some female dancers have less quadriceps strength than the average athlete, and some technique or warm-up classes do not provide adequate quadriceps training. So get working on improving thigh strength!

Wall Sit

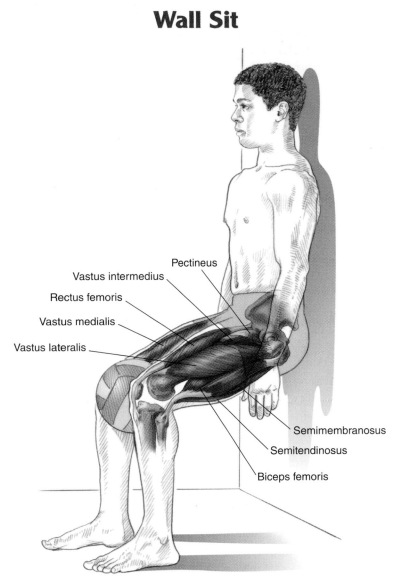

Pectineus

Vastus intermedius

Rectus femoris

Vastus medialis

Vastus lateralis

Semimembranosus

Semitendinosus

Biceps femoris

Execution

1. Stand with your back against a wall. Bring your heels away from the wall about 2 feet (60 cm). Lean into the wall and place a small ball between the knees. Inhale to prepare.

2. Exhale and perform a parallel demi-plié by sliding down the wall. Feel your weight placed evenly throughout your foot. Reemphasize pressure through the heel if necessary. Contract the adductors into the ball.

3. Hold that position for 2 to 4 counts, creating an isometric contraction. Slide up the wall to return. Repeat with a deeper demi-plié, taking the thighs parallel with the floor. Hold 2 to 4 counts and then slide up the wall. Repeat the series 4 to 6 times.

SAFETY TIP All natural curves of the spine should remain intact. Reemphasize neutral spine, not a posterior tilt. To reduce compression forces in the knee joint, avoid pliés deeper than 90 degrees of knee flexion.

Muscles Involved

Biceps femoris, vastus medialis, vastus intermedius, vastus lateralis, adductor longus, adductor brevis, adductor magnus, gracilis, pectineus, rectus femoris, semimembranosus, semitendinosus

Dance Focus

You will notice the challenge increase when you bend the knees a little deeper. While parallel or turned out, grande plié can create compression under the patella; it's a wonderful quadriceps exercise if your quads are strong enough! As the plié deepens, the patella moves from its safe vertical alignment into a stronger force deeper into the femur. Know that grande plié can put approximately 7 times your body weight directly into the knee joint. Multiply your weight by 7, and imagine how much that is with every grande plié. Maybe grande plié should be used a little later in the ballet technique class; this would allow more time for the legs to get warmed up. You will need impeccable quadriceps strength to execute the hinge of the Horton modern technique, where your body weight is back and your knees and thighs maintain your weight and stability. The grande cambré lunge in classical ballet calls for deep knee flexion and a strong quadriceps contraction. Various contemporary styles of choreography might require bearing all of your weight on your knees while turning. If you are using this exercise to emphasize alignment of the knees over the toes, 4 to 6 repetitions might be enough; but if you are looking to gain strength, repeat this exercise to fatigue.

Hamstring Curl

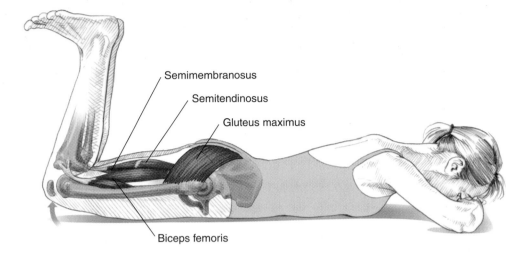

Semimembranosus

Semitendinosus

Gluteus maximus

Biceps femoris

Execution

1. While lying facedown, rest your forehead on your hands. Legs are together and parallel. Bend both knees simultaneously to 90 degrees and flex the ankles, keeping knees and ankles touching. Inhale to prepare.

2. On exhalation, engage the deep abdominals and lengthen through the spine. Lift both thighs slightly off the floor, engaging the hamstrings and gluteus maximus. Hold for a count of 4.

3. Lengthen through the front of the hips. Allow the thighs to hover over the floor just about an inch. Inhale to return with control. Repeat 10 to 12 times.

⚠ **SAFETY TIP** Reinforce the deep abdominals to protect the lower spine. This exercise will also engage stabilizing muscles along the spine. Resist arching the lower back—work to stay in your natural supported pelvic position.

Muscles Involved

Biceps femoris, semitendinosus, semimembranosus, gluteus maximus

Dance Focus

The hamstrings provide support in perfect body placement, but they also flex the knee and extend the hip. They have a two-joint action! Some dancers have hyperextended knees, meaning the knees can continue past full extension because of laxity and a posterior gravitational torque. If you activate the hamstrings a little sooner, they can assist in controlling hyperextension. The hamstrings work for you each time you execute coupé, passé, and attitude positions in ballet as well as barrel turns and stag leaps in jazz. The biceps femoris also assists with turnout; you should feel it contract with attitude derrière and turned-out arabesque. Try to think about hip disassociation: Move your thighs to the back as far as you can without any movement in your lower spine. Challenge yourself to move the thighs against the resistance of the pelvis and spine.

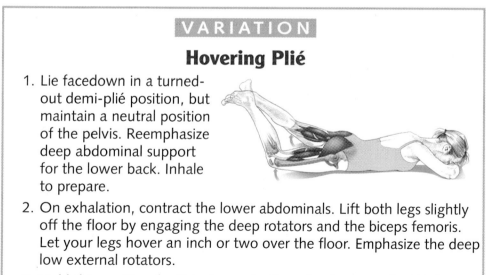

VARIATION

Hovering Plié

1. Lie facedown in a turned-out demi-plié position, but maintain a neutral position of the pelvis. Reemphasize deep abdominal support for the lower back. Inhale to prepare.

2. On exhalation, contract the lower abdominals. Lift both legs slightly off the floor by engaging the deep rotators and the biceps femoris. Let your legs hover an inch or two over the floor. Emphasize the deep low external rotators.

3. Hold this position for 2 to 4 counts, then slowly return the thighs to the floor with control. Repeat 10 to 12 times.

Hamstring Lift

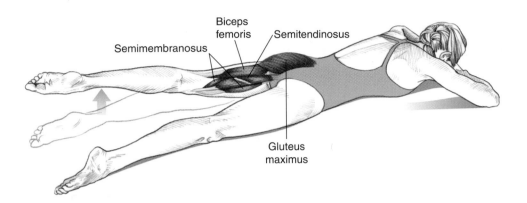

Semimembranosus
Biceps femoris
Semitendinosus
Gluteus maximus

Execution

1. Lie facedown with your hands under your forehead and legs slightly turned out (you will later repeat the exercise in parallel). Elongate and lengthen through the entire spine. Inhale to prepare.

2. As you exhale, focus on the contraction of the hamstrings with the deep abdominals and elevate one leg; only lift the leg approximately 10 degrees but maintain a neutral position of the pelvis.

3. Feel the hamstrings and abdominals working together against the resistance of the pelvis wanting to move into an anterior tilt. Hold for 4 counts. As you inhale, slowly return the leg with control. Repeat 12 times turned out and in parallel.

⚠️ **SAFETY TIP** Activate the abdominals and then lift with the hamstrings. Don't release in the lower back, letting your momentum carry your leg up without control! This will eventually wear down the lower segments of your spine and tighten the lower back, causing an overuse injury.

Muscles Involved

Biceps femoris, semitendinosus, semimembranosus, gluteus maximus

Dance Focus

You have learned that your hamstrings originate at the sit bones. Because of their connection with the pelvis, weakness can cause ineffectiveness in pelvic alignment. Think about your plumb line; weakness of the hamstring complex will allow your pelvis to tilt forward, moving you out of your optimal body placement. A firm balance between the lift of the abdominals and strength of the hamstrings facilitates a balanced pelvis and lower back. You need to have extreme flexibility in your hamstrings, but it is also important to maintain strength. Your hamstrings help you with arabesque and powerful jumps. Practice leg lifts to the back with a new awareness of engaging abdominals with hamstrings to give you added support. As the arabesque goes higher, maintain that low abdominal support and shift your upper torso forward, emphasizing spinal extension in the upper back and chest while maintaining that abdomen–hamstring connection. The supported hamstring lift variation supports the spine and allows

you to isolate the hamstrings and gluteus maximus without engaging the spine extensor muscles. The back of your thighs are fast-twitch muscles that move your knee and hip through all levels of rapidly changing dance movements. Sometimes the tops of your thighs will overpower your hamstrings. Keep working on strengthening your hamstrings.

VARIATION
Supported Hamstring Lift

1. Lay your upper body over a table with your feet on the floor. The table's edge is firm against the hip flexors and your hands are under your forehead. Inhale on the preparation.

2. On exhalation, engage the deep abdomen and lift one leg off the floor with a straight knee, contracting the hamstrings and gluteus maximus. Do not allow your pelvis or lower back to move. Hold for 4 counts and return slowly. Repeat 10 to 12 times each side.

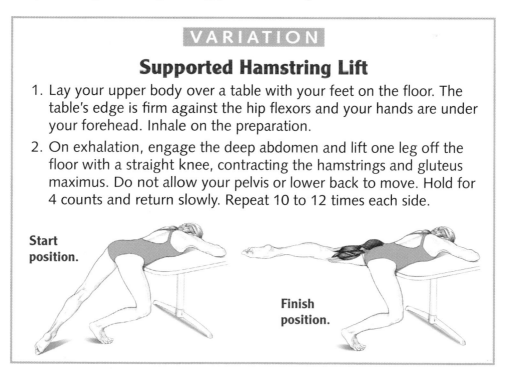

Start position.

Finish position.

Side Scissor

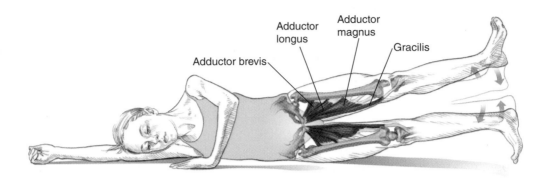

Execution

1. Lie on your right side with your head on your right arm extended overhead and left arm on the floor in front of you. Both legs are extended. Maintain a neutral spine, and maintain lift in the waist on both sides of your body. Stack knees directly on top of each other. Inhale to prepare.

2. On exhalation, turn out and lift the top leg, then turn out and lift the bottom leg. Engage your core musculature to maintain a secure trunk. If balance is compromised, bring the legs forward slightly by flexing the hips. Remain in neutral for your spine and pelvis.

3. Execute small inner-thigh pulses. Feel the pelvic floor, deep transversus abdominis, and adductors contracting. Perform the pulses for 10 to 12 counts before slowly returning with control. Repeat the series 3 to 5 times. Increase tempo with each set.

⚠ **SAFETY TIP** The bottom leg must remain turned out to avoid compression of the greater trochanter against the floor. Maintain a deep abdominal contraction for spinal stability.

Muscles Involved

Adductor longus, adductor brevis, adductor magnus, gracilis

Dance Focus

Most dancers seem to spend more time stretching the adductors than strengthening. The gluteus medius and the adductors work together to provide more pelvic stability. Visualize the originations and insertions of the inner-thigh muscles; they line the medial portion of the femur to connect with the pelvis. Even though they lose effectiveness at leg heights above approximately 50 degrees, they are very active in flexion, extension, and of course adduction at lower levels. Irish dancers use the adductors frequently when the legs are crossed to give the audience an illusion of seeing only one knee from the front. The same principle applies when performing bourrées in ballet: The adductors remain contracted to cross the legs. Fourth and fifth position in ballet calls for the inner thighs to be contracted for pelvic stability, and jumping combinations with leg beats require strong inner thighs as well. Practice the side scissor slowly and with control, then increase the speed of the leg beats to improve precision.

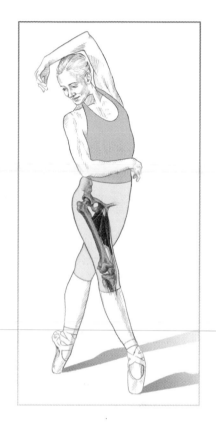

Assisted Développé

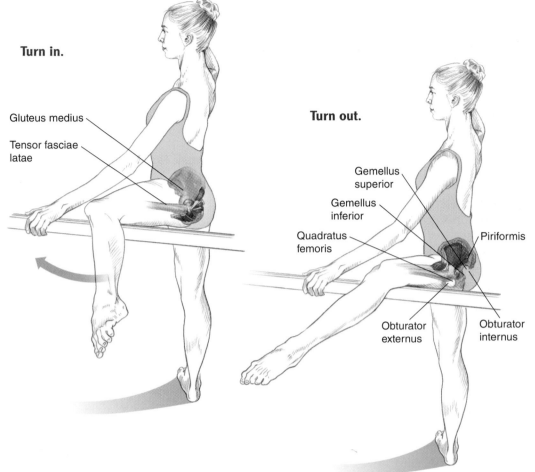

Turn in.

Gluteus medius

Tensor fasciae latae

Turn out.

Gemellus superior

Gemellus inferior

Quadratus femoris

Piriformis

Obturator externus

Obturator internus

Execution

1. Stand with your left hand on the barre. The inside (left) leg lies over the barre beneath your knee in à la seconde. Organize your placement: Turn out your standing (right) leg and place your right hand on your shoulder; your left thigh, which is on the barre, must be higher than 90 degrees.

2. Turn the left thigh inward and outward, noting the hip hike with turn-in and the deep low rotators on the external rotation. Repeat 4 times.

3. After completing the last turnout of the thigh, begin to extend or unfold the knee by lifting the lower leg, not by allowing your thigh to bear down into the barre. Keep your leg on the barre while engaging the deep hip external rotators and the iliopsoas.

⚠ **SAFETY TIP** Avoid twisting in the knee of the supporting leg.

Muscles Involved

Internal rotation: anterior fibers of the gluteus medius and minimus, tensor fasciae latae

External rotation: Obturator internus, obturator externus, piriformis, quadratus femoris, gemellus inferior, gemellus superior

Knee extension: Rectus femoris, vastus medialis, vastus intermedius, vastus lateralis, sartorius

Dance Focus

So, you have figured out how to get your thigh to your chest but then you start to extend the knee and the femur starts to drop. You feel this intense overuse of the quadriceps. Remember, once you have contracted the quadriceps, they cannot help you to elevate your leg any higher—your développé is done! Visualize your femur glued to your ribs; increase the deep iliopsoas contraction to keep your thigh glued to the ribs, and keep the deep low rotators contracting very strongly to maintain turnout of the thigh. There is a spiraling effect of the thigh in the hip socket throughout the movement. It might help to remember to aim your sit bone down toward the floor and let the outside of the thigh rotate downward as well. Now, just lift the lower leg; visualize the tibia, foot, and ankle floating up; and let

the quadriceps contraction pull to elevate the lower leg. It's important to keep the iliopsoas contracting and the deep rotators contracting to provide support to the femur above 90 degrees. Remind yourself to keep turning out the back of your thigh. You will also notice the supporting-side gluteus medius help to stabilize your pelvis. Let them all work together to give you an amazing développé.

Descending Battement

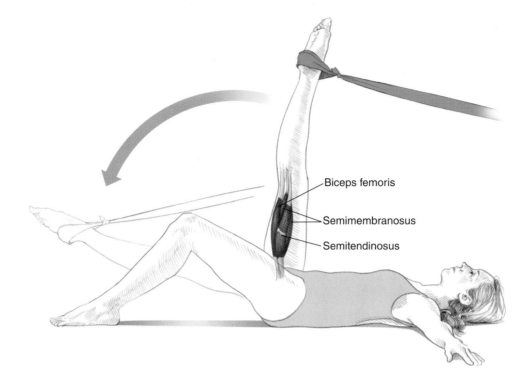

Biceps femoris

Semimembranosus

Semitendinosus

Execution

1. Lie on your back. Your left knee is bent and your foot is on the floor. Your right leg begins at 90 degrees of hip flexion and turned out; the knee is fully extended. Secure one end of an elastic band around the forefoot; the other end should be stabilized high and behind you. Inhale to prepare.

2. On exhalation, engage the deep abdominals to secure your lower back. Bring your leg down with control against the resistance of the band as if returning from grande battement.

3. Inhale as the leg goes up. Feel as though you are lifting the leg with the upper inner thigh. Increase speed on the upward phase and keep it slow and controlled against the resistance on the downward phase. Reemphasize trunk control with each battement. Repeat 10 to 12 times.

⚠ **SAFETY TIP** Avoid anterior pelvic tilt or lateral pelvic tilt to maintain pelvic security. Move only the thigh, not the spine or pelvis.

Muscles Involved

Biceps femoris, semimembranosus, semitendinosus

Dance Focus

Using control when coming down from high kicks, grande jetés, or traveling leaps will give your work the look of defying gravity. Use the band to focus on the concentric contraction of the hamstrings as the leg comes down. Allow the band to give you assistance as the leg goes back up and maintain the eccentric lengthening through the hamstrings and gluteus maximus. Fight to hold your turnout through the entire range; it will keep the hip from elevating. At the top of the battement, feel as though your leg could lengthen; hover and lift before it slowly begins to come down. Maintain an anchored pelvis and reaffirm the principle of hip disassociation. Remind yourself to turn out the back of the thigh. This exer-

cise can also be repeated while lying on your side for à la seconde. While executing these two exercises, close your eyes for a couple of repetitions to focus on deep transversus abdominis work hugging your spine like a corset. This is the support you need to be able to move your legs freely.

Variation: side-lying battement.

ANKLES AND FEET

Strong and balanced feet provide the foundation for the whole body. Knowledge of lower-leg alignment together with core and pelvic strength will give your feet the power you need in order to be quick and fearless. As a dancer, you need to have a basic understanding of accurate alignment and muscle action to improve your technique. There are 26 bones in your foot and 34 joints, thus creating multiple movement possibilities. When bearing weight, any joint movement has a direct relation to the other joints in your feet. You must be able to dance as a unit with all joints working in harmony.

Modern, jazz, ballroom, Irish, and most folk dance styles require similar foot and ankle movements. You must be able to travel quickly on your feet and rise up on the balls of your feet and the tips of your toes. You might need to run and jump in heels or pivot and push with bare feet. Tappers, cloggers, and flamenco dancers do a lot of challenging percussive footwork that requires intense power. Turning, jumping, pointing, relevé, and plié are basic skills needed for all dance techniques. Each style requires unusual positions of the feet, not to mention particular footwear that is used more for aesthetic appearance than for true support. Classical ballet requires extreme range of motion for pointe work, but this chapter applies to all styles and the importance of education in anatomy. It's helpful to know the supporting structures that keep your arches alive and strong. It's important to know where ankle stability comes from to reduce the risk of ankle sprains. It's also useful to understand basic muscle movement so you can benefit from strengthening exercises. Quick and fearless feet don't just happen—they need training, care, and maintenance.

Bony Anatomy

The malleoli (ankle bones) are the projections at the base of the tibia and fibula bones. The ankle bones are sites for some of the ankle's strong supporting ligaments. The talus bone fits snugly in between the ankle bones and is somewhat responsible for transmitting your weight to the rest of your foot. It meets the calcaneous (heel bone) in the back and the navicular bone in the front (figure 8.1). The heel bone provides the base for the attachment of the Achilles tendon, and the navicular bone provides the base for the tibialis posterior tendon. Both tendons activate to point the foot and ankle. Along the middle region of the foot are three cuneiform bones and the cuboid, which meet the five metatarsal bones. This middle region gives you mobility for a beautiful

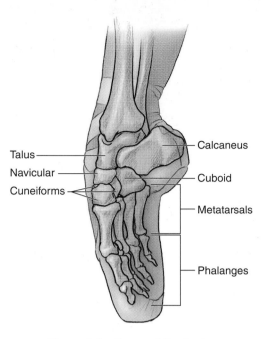

Talus

Navicular

Cuneiforms

Calcaneus

Cuboid

Metatarsals

Phalanges

Figure 8.1   Bones of the foot.

point and firmness for support. The metatarsals meet the phalanges, or toe bones; flexibility in these joints is needed for the best possible half pointe. All of the bones in your feet are connected by ligaments and muscle tendons, which provide support. For the rest of the text we break down the foot into segments. The forefoot consists of the phalanges and metatarsals; the midfoot consists of the navicular, the three cuneiforms, and the cuboid. The rearfoot is composed of the calcaneous and the talus.

The bones in your feet are not organized in a flat formation. The inside border forms a long arch, which is referred to as the medial longitudinal arch. When instructors say, "Don't roll in," they are usually referring to this arch of your foot flattening out. Even though the outside border of your foot is on the floor, it also forms a lateral longitudinal arch. As long as some of your weight is placed along the outside arch, the inside arch can activate and lift. The transverse arch runs across from the inside to the outside. This arch creates the striking high instep that so many dancers work for. The arches of your feet are supported by the bones in your feet. They need to be strong and active to support your weight, jumping activities, balance poses, and twisting movements. The arches are also supported by fascia and ligaments. The fascia is a very tough band of connective tissue on the sole of your foot. It runs between your forefoot and your heel. Maintaining strength in your feet will reduce the risk of developing plantar fasciitis, or inflammation of the fascia. Weakness and tightness within the arches will cause overuse of the fascia. You can avoid this overuse syndrome by maintaining strength and flexibility in your feet.

Foot and Ankle Motion

The ankle joint is capable of pointing and flexing, which in medical terms are plantar flexion and dorsiflexion. At the highest point of your relevé is a tiny bit of sideways movement capability, which sometimes helps when you're trying to maintain a balanced pose en pointe. The talus sits snugly in a box-like space. In plié the talus moves slightly to the back, where it fits tight and provides stability. In some cases, when the demi-plié is too deep, the talus can come into contact with the base of the tibia. This can cause pain and swelling and eventually lead to bone spurs. Maintaining strength and eccentric muscle control in your legs will help keep your plié from causing this impingement.

During demi-pointe, the talus moves slightly forward out of the security of its space, causing instability. The inversion press, winging, and relevé with ball exercises in this chapter (pages 156, 158, and 160) focus on ankle support. Some dancers struggle with a fully pointed position because the back of the talus bone may have an abnormal bony projection that comes into contact with the heel bone. This unfortunate posterior impingement limits full-height relevé, creates an unstable ankle, and leads to a weight-back situation. When you are unable to transfer your center of gravity completely over your half-pointe or full-pointe position, your body weight will remain too far back. This incorrect weight placement can create overuse and stress injuries. Working with your weight back compromises balance and overworks the lower-leg musculature due to compensation.

The subtalar joint in the rearfoot is located where the talus and calcaneous meet. This joint allows for adequate pronation in plié and supination in relevé, whether you are working parallel or turned out. Pronation refers to the inside arch and talus moving downward, while supination is just the opposite. The inside arch and talus move slightly upward. This movement is needed for propulsion in relevé and jumps as well as shock absorption on landing. But excessive pronation leads to rolling in and undue stress on your arch. Rolling in sometimes occurs from forcing the turnout at the feet and not using the deep hip external rotators and adductors.

Good movement through the rearfoot dictates needed movement for the midfoot. For example, with plié the inner portion of the heel bone will slightly move inward so the talus can move slightly inward. This small movement has to happen to open the joints of the midfoot. When the midfoot joints loosen, flexibility occurs for shock absorption and a soft plié. The exact opposite occurs for relevé. The heel and talus will slightly lift so the midfoot joints can tighten. The tightness provides a firm arch for relevé. Strengthening the muscles of the midfoot region will allow excellent weight transfer onto the first, second, and third metatarsals when executing relevé. The arches can then become rigid to help stabilize the relevé.

The joints where the metatarsals meet the phalanges must have significant strength and flexibility for toe-off during jumping movements. There must be an eccentric lengthening under the toes on relevé to provide an adequate base. The eccentric lengthening allows the small muscles under the forefoot and toes to be long but strong and active. Even in a standing position, your toes should be lengthened and your arch musculature activated to provide a firm anchor. The first exercise, doming (page 152), improves arch support and reduces the weakness caused by curling of the toes.

Support Ligaments

You probably know a dancer who has had an ankle sprain, a very common injury. Numerous ligaments are in the foot and ankle, but we will look at five of the ligaments providing support. The medial ligament complex is called the deltoid, which originates on the medial malleolus and fans out to attach on the navicular, talus, and calcaneous bones. This is an extremely strong combination of ligaments that provide vital stability. The spring ligament is also located on the medial side of the foot and connects the calcaneous with the navicular bone; it has the principal job of providing a sling for the talus, which aids in supporting the weight of the body. Weakness or lengthening along this ligament can cause flattening of the foot.

On the outside of your ankle are three ligaments that together provide stability. These ligaments are not as strong as the deltoid and are usually the first ligaments to be injured in a lateral ankle sprain. A lateral ankle sprain refers to an injury in which the sole of the foot turns inward, damaging the supporting ligaments. The anterior talofibular ligament runs between the talus and the fibula; when in relevé this ligament moves into a vertical stable position. The calcaneofibular and posterior talofibular ligaments, as you might guess by their names, run between the calcaneous, talus, and fibula bones and also help to maintain critical alignment and ankle stability.

Muscle Mechanics

Foot and ankle action is allowed by 12 intrinsic muscles located within the foot itself and 12 extrinsic muscles that originate outside of the foot and have multiple actions. The gastrocnemius is the large muscle that originates behind your knee and inserts in the calcaneous bone by way of the Achilles tendon (figure 8.2). Underneath the gastrocnemius is the soleus, which also connects into the Achilles tendon. The gastrocnemius is a two-joint muscle, meaning it can flex your knee and point your foot. The soleus can also point your foot and plays a role in maintaining your balance. Together these are the two primary movers for relevé and pointing. The soleus is valuable for rising from half pointe to full pointe and in securing control on landings from jumps. The seated soleus pump exercise (page 162) offers two variations for soleus-specific strengthening.

Other muscles that originate in back of the tibia or fibula and assist with plantar flexion and inversion are the tibialis posterior, flexor digitorum longus, and flexor hallucis longus. The tibialis posterior inserts mainly into the navicular bone and provides added support for the inner arch. The flexor digitorum longus inserts into digits (toes) 2 through 5.

The flexor hallucis longus tendon deserves more attention. This muscle originates along the back of the fibula. It runs along the back of your lower leg through a small tunnel beneath the inside ankle bone, and it inserts into

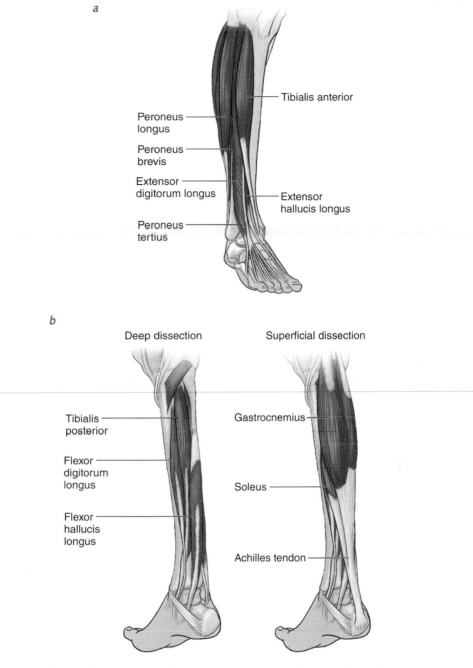

a

Tibialis anterior

Peroneus longus

Peroneus brevis

Extensor digitorum longus

Extensor hallucis longus

Peroneus tertius

b

Deep dissection

Superficial dissection

Tibialis posterior

Flexor digitorum longus

Flexor hallucis longus

Gastrocnemius

Soleus

Achilles tendon

Figure 8.2 Muscles of the lower leg and foot: *(a)* front; *(b)* back.

the base of the big toe. This tendon has many jobs: flexion of the big toe, push-off power for jumps, and support for the inner arch. Repetitive overuse of the flexor hallucis longus tendon with pointing and relevé can lead to discomfort and inflammation, which has been called dancer's tendinitis. This tendon can also become trapped within the tunnel and cause triggering, which can lead to fraying or tearing. It is imperative to strengthen all of the muscles responsible for pointing to avoid overuse of the flexor hallucis longus tendon. These exercises are also included in this chapter.

Muscles along the lateral lower leg are the peroneals; they originate at the upper fibula. One inserts into the fifth metatarsal and one continues under the foot to insert into the first metatarsal. Their job is to provide strength for the outside of your lower legs and reduce the risk of lateral ankle sprains. Along the front of the tibia is the tibialis anterior, extensor hallucis longus, and extensor digitorum longus. These muscles pull the toes upward and flex and invert the ankle. All of the extrinsic muscles work to hug your lower leg to your ankle and provide support.

The soles of your feet are also layered with supportive muscles (figure 8.3). These intrinsic muscles connect the heel with tarsal and metatarsal bones and are solely responsible for lengthening the toes. The small muscle supporting the inner arch that runs from the big toe to the inside of the heel is called the abductor hallucis; you can train this muscle to activate to provide strength to the inner-arch area. The big-toe abduction exercise (page 154) can assist you in strengthening this muscle. Deep muscles are also located between the metatarsals and phalanges; weakness within these intrinsic muscles can cause clawing of the toes. The toes must stay lengthened for push-off skills for jumping.

Dance-Focused Exercise

While executing the next series of exercises, visualize the muscles hugging your ankle for support. Each time you flex or demi-plié, visualize the talus bone securely in its space for support. Think about energy along all of your arches. Each time you point your foot, align the second and third metatarsals with the tibia bone for a perfect line. Remember to lengthen under the toes to avoid clawing; this will give you a wider base during half-pointe. A wider base will promote a better platform for balancing. Try to repeat all exercises with various speeds and work with control throughout the entire range of motion.

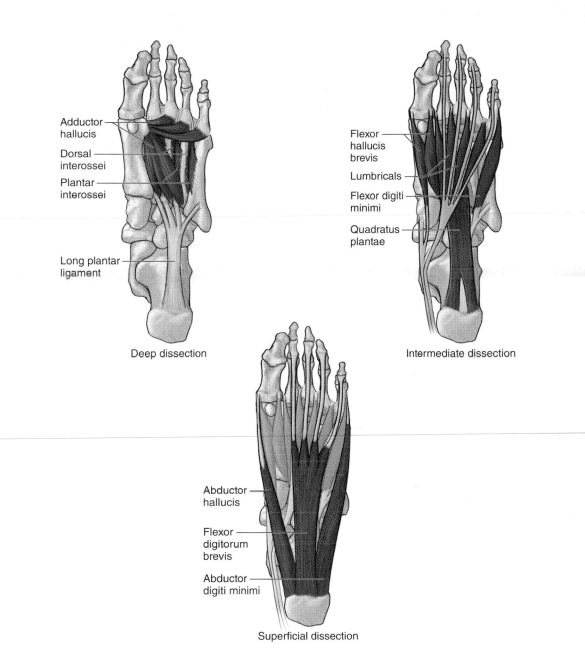

Adductor
hallucis

Dorsal
interossei

Plantar
interossei

Long plantar
ligament

Deep dissection

Flexor
hallucis
brevis

Lumbricals

Flexor digiti
minimi

Quadratus
plantae

Intermediate dissection

Abductor
hallucis

Flexor
digitorum
brevis

Abductor
digiti minimi

Superficial dissection

Figure 8.3 Intrinsic muscles of the foot.

Doming

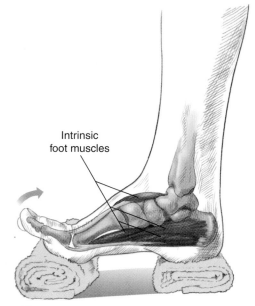

Intrinsic foot muscles

Toes up.

Toes down.

Execution

1. Begin while seated. Place your forefoot on a small towel roll and place your heel on another small towel roll. Use the rolls to balance the placement of your foot evenly across the metatarsal heads and the heel.

2. Lift all toes upward without lifting the forefoot off the towel roll. Reestablish equal weight placement. Lengthen under the toes as you begin to press them toward the floor.

3. Engage the deep intrinsic muscles throughout your arch and draw the metatarsal heads toward the heel. The movement is initiated from the metatarsal phalangeal joint until the toes are on the floor. Do not curl the toes; allow the intrinsic musculature to draw the metatarsal heads toward the heel. Repeat 15 times, working up to 30.

Muscles Involved

Intrinsic foot muscles

Dance Focus

Numerous small muscles are located along the soles of your feet; they play a significant role in pointing your feet, in moving from half pointe to full pointe, and in pushing off for jumps. Some of your choreographic requirements can really take a toll on your feet. The intrinsic muscles along with the anatomy of the bones support the various arches in your feet and help resist curling the toes. The intrinsic muscle group must feel active in order to create support. Close your eyes and focus on this specific area of your feet. Visualize the strong fascia along with the numerous muscle fibers contracting to provide control. Whether you are dancing barefoot, in pointe shoes, or in character shoes, the

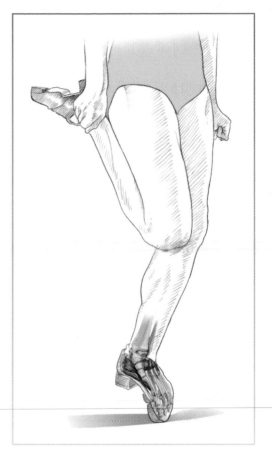

intrinsic musculature must be strong to give you the power and spring needed for jumps and pointe work. Some warm-up and basic technique classes provide limited education in this specific area of your foot. Again, it is up to you to maintain the quality of your arches by taking extra time to strengthen your feet.

Big-Toe Abduction

Abductor
hallucis

Execution

1. Begin seated. Place your feet on the floor, emphasizing equal weight placement between the metatarsal heads and heel.

2. Try to open the big toe away from the other toes. Hold for 2 to 4 counts and then slowly return. Feel the boost of the medial arch as the big toe moves.

3. Repeat 10 to 12 times to feel the muscle contraction. Work up to 3 sets of 12.

Muscles Involved

Abductor hallucis

Dance Focus

The medial arch should have a beautiful dome-shaped arch; the lack of an arch is typically what instructors focus on when cueing you to not roll in. Weakness in the abductor hallucis and laxity in the ligaments over time will lead to a flattened medial arch. Exaggerating turnout from the feet instead of working turnout from the hips creates a collapse of the medial arch, which can lead to numerous injuries. Placing equal weight along the lateral arch will assist in organizing the muscles to provide the correct spring needed along the medial arch. All dance styles

require constant shifting of body weight, causing the arches to change form; your arches must be strong enough to tolerate these changes. You can use this muscle to provide support for your medial longitudinal arch whether you are dancing barefoot, en pointe, or in character shoes. The medial arch needs to become rigid and secure in relevé, lengthened but active in plié, and alive for balancing.

Inversion Press

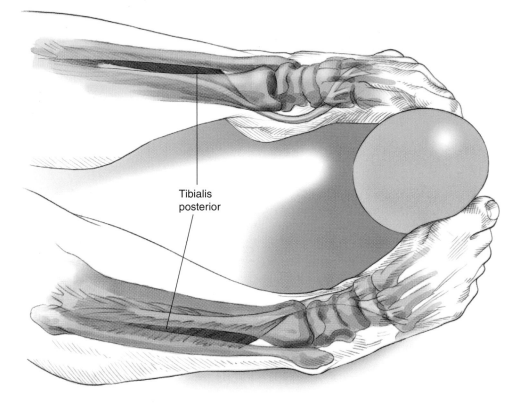

Tibialis
posterior

Execution

1. Sit with both knees bent and soles of the feet parallel on the floor. Place a medium-size ball between your feet in the area of the fore-foot.

2. With the heels of both feet remaining on the floor, begin to press the forefeet into the ball, lifting the inner arches of both feet.

3. As you move your forefeet inward, press into the ball and maintain an isometric contraction for 2 to 4 counts. Repeat 10 to 12 times, working up to 3 sets.

⚠️ **SAFETY TIP** Avoid overstretching of the outside of the ankle. Use this exercise to focus on the arch-lifting aspect and strengthen the inside of the ankle.

Muscles Involved

Tibialis posterior

Dance Focus

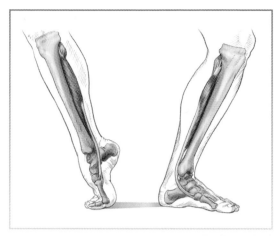

The tibialis posterior supports the medial arch and helps resist pronation. Although the tibialis anterior also will contract, focus on the tibialis posterior pulling the foot inward and lifting the arch. The talus bone needs to stay in a relatively neutral position to provide the most stability for the foot and ankle. There is some natural pronation with each plié and some natural supination with relevé, but excessive pronation leads to numerous overuse injuries. In relevé, feel deep support of this tendon by visualizing its many insertions into the navicular bone and tarsal bones. Maintaining strength of the tibialis posterior tendon will help provide stability for the foot and ankle when landing from jumps as well. The foot begins to articulate as it meets the floor from a jump; the tibialis posterior can help your arch feel lifted, giving you smoother, more cushioned landings. Vary the tempo with this exercise: Move into inversion quickly and return slowly, then reverse the tempo change. This will provide changes in velocity of the muscle contraction, which will simulate challenges and changes in choreography.

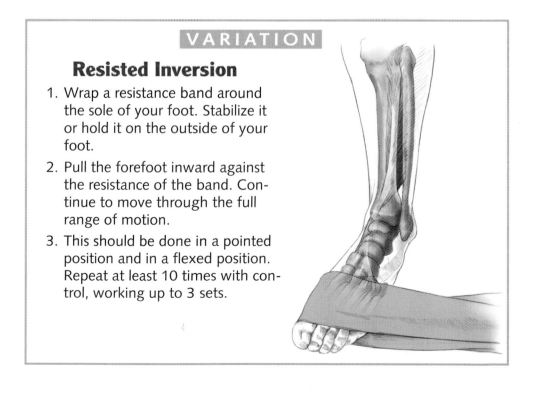

VARIATION

Resisted Inversion

1. Wrap a resistance band around the sole of your foot. Stabilize it or hold it on the outside of your foot.

2. Pull the forefoot inward against the resistance of the band. Continue to move through the full range of motion.

3. This should be done in a pointed position and in a flexed position. Repeat at least 10 times with control, working up to 3 sets.

Winging

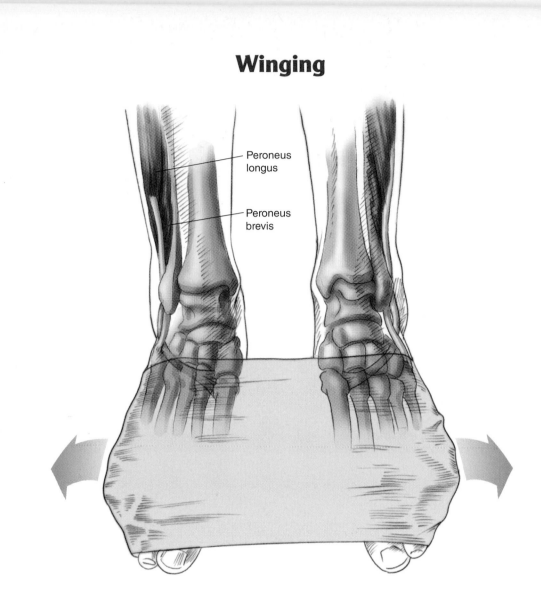

Peroneus longus

Peroneus brevis

Execution

1. Sit with an elastic band tied together and wrapped around the forefoot.

2. Breathe comfortably and push the forefeet outward against the resistance of the band.

3. Repeat this 10 to 12 times in a pointed position and in a flexed position, working up to 3 sets. Reemphasize control through the full range of motion.

⚠ **SAFETY TIP** Avoid creating torque through the knees; isolate the movement to the feet and the ankles.

Muscles Involved

Peroneus longus, peroneus brevis

Dance Focus

The combination of the muscles along the lateral lower leg and the tibialis posterior (mentioned previously) give you support through the effect of a stirrup. With excessive range of motion in relevé, you need security to avoid twisting your ankle and damaging the ligaments. Without adequate strength of the peroneus muscles, the ankle will continue to twist, leaving the joint unstable. This goes for every style of dance movement and with every pointing position, relevé, push-off, and landing from a jump. Visualize a stirrup holding your ankle secure so you are free to point your foot through extreme ranges. The majority of injuries that

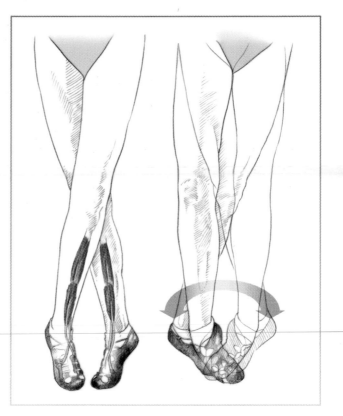

dancers sustain are to the lower leg and foot; it is imperative that you strengthen the ankles to reduce the risk of traumatic injury.

Relevé With Ball

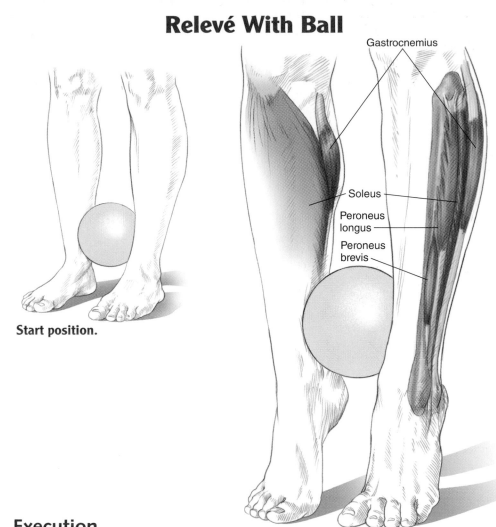

Gastrocnemius

Soleus

Peroneus
longus

Peroneus
brevis

Start position.

Execution

1. While facing the barre with your legs parallel, place a small ball between the heels. Reorganize your trunk to maintain neutral postural alignment. Align the tibia over the second toe.

2. Begin to relevé with gentle pressure against the ball and align the middle of the talus over the second toe.

3. Hold for 2 to 4 counts before returning with control. Repeat this 15 to 30 times.

⚠ SAFETY TIP To improve ankle support and control, avoid sickling the ankle. Focus on relevé directly over the second and third metatarsals.

Muscles Involved

Gastrocnemius, soleus, peroneus longus, peroneus brevis

Dance Focus

Exercising against your own body weight will give you even more awareness and dynamic challenge. Use this exercise of relevé with the ball to reinforce the relationship of the talus and the heel during relevé. Feel the lateral and posterior lower leg giving you incredible support. Try it one time allowing the heels to supinate just a small amount; notice that you are unable to hold the ball and notice how the ankles feel really unstable. Any traveling movements involving pivots require power in order to push off in a horizontal direction; you will need strength in the lateral lower leg combined with strength in the gastrocnemius and soleus to execute the movement. The muscles along the outside of your lower leg also provide strength and

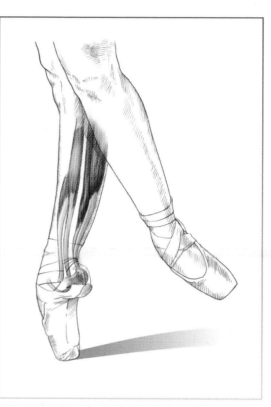

the ability to wing your feet in a coupé-type position. Remember to control your movements on the landing. You have a tendency to use all of your efforts and momentum on the upward phase and then let gravity bring you down. Loss of control on the down phase puts you at risk for injury. You must have adequate strength to be able to recover from an extreme off-balance accident to avoid injury.

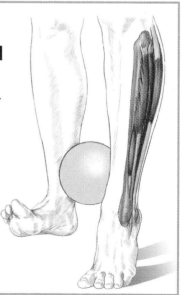

VARIATION

Eccentrics With Ball

1. Repeat this exercise, except after relevé, release the forefoot and dorsiflex the foot. Continue to hold the ball.

2. Slowly lower your body back down with one foot. Go up with two feet; return down with one. Reemphasize control on the way down.

3. Maintain pressure of the ball between the heels. Alternate legs and repeat 10 to 12 times, working up to 3 sets. Focus on eccentric strength of the lower legs as if you are landing from a jump.

Seated Soleus Pump

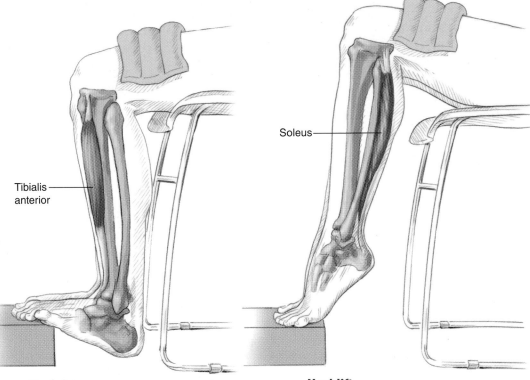

Heel drop.   **Heel lift.**

Execution

1. While seated in a chair with your legs parallel, place your forefeet on a ledge while your heels remain on the floor. Check that your knees are at a 90-degree angle, and place a small 5-pound weight (about 2 kg) on top of each thigh to give you more resistance.

2. Begin relevé into full range of motion, aligning the second toe with the center of the talus. Lengthen under the toes and widen the metatarsals.

3. Return to starting position with control. Repeat 15 to 30 times, working up to 3 sets. Engage the deep soleus.

⚠️ **SAFETY TIP** To maintain control and alignment of the tibia bone and second metatarsal, avoid sickling the ankles.

Muscles Involved

Dorsiflexion: Tibialis anterior

Relevé: Soleus

Dance Focus

Landing from jumps with control cannot be emphasized enough. Strengthening the lower-leg muscles to control your body when coming down from relevé, small jumps, and grande allegro movements will give you the look of defying gravity and injury. Soleus pumps require you to maintain muscular strength as the muscle lengthens. When your toes first make contact with the floor, there must be a significant amount of articulation to cushion the landing and a significant amount of muscular endurance to support your body weight against gravity. The gastrocnemius typically fires more on the landing phase of jumping, so strengthening the soleus will provide

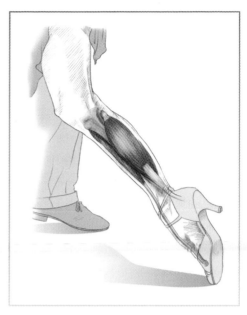

better assistance for the gastrocnemius. The soleus muscle also contains more type I (slow-twitch) muscle fibers, which helps provide awareness for balance and security of the lower leg on the ankle. The soleus helps keep your body from falling forward when standing and helps maintain balance whether you are dancing in character shoes or en pointe. Remember that because of the higher content of type I fibers, the soleus is more resistant to fatigue; you will need to increase your repetitions to improve strength.

VARIATION

Resistance Band Pump

1. Sit on the edge of a table or hang your leg over the barre so the barre hits just above the back of your knee. Wrap a resistance band around the metatarsal heads. Keeping the toes covered, hold the band from above.

2. Without activating your quadriceps, push your foot into plantar flexion against the resistance of the band. You don't even have to point your toes; just point the ankle.

3. Alternate flexing and pointing at the ankle with emphasis on the deep soleus contraction. Repeat 30 times or more, working up to 3 sets.

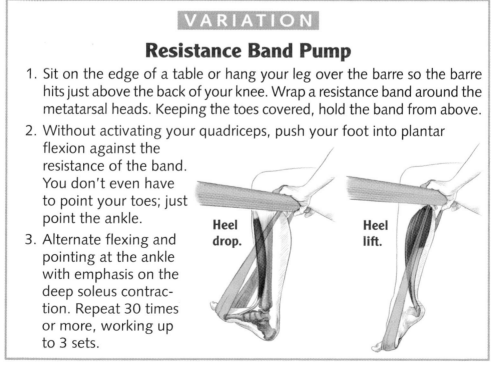

Heel drop.

Heel lift.

Toe Isolations

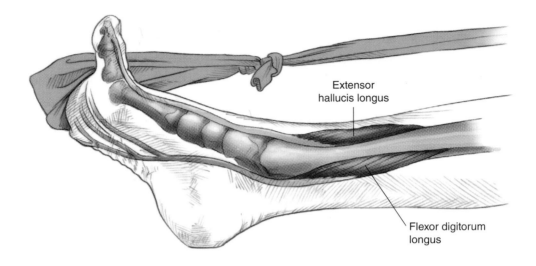

Extensor
hallucis longus

Flexor digitorum
longus

Execution

1. Sit on the floor with a resistance band wrapped around toes 2 through 5. Extend your knee, holding the ends of the band in your hands.

2. Allow the big toe to remain in dorsiflexion as you point the other toes against the resistance of the band.

3. Repeat this 10 to 12 times with the ankle in a pointed position and the big toe dorsiflexed. Move toes 2 through 5 through the full range of motion. You can try this one toe at a time as well to isolate the movement even more.

⚠ **SAFETY TIP** Resist the band's tendency to curl and compress the toes. Try to lengthen the toes as you point them to work through the intrinsic muscle group of the forefoot.

Muscles Involved

Big toe: Extensor hallucis longus

Toes 2 through 5: Flexor digitorum longus

Dance Focus

Toe isolations make you aware of the need to use toes 2 through 5 because of their role in pushing you off the floor. You might have a tendency to overuse the big toe and the flexor hallucis longus for the push-off. Although the big toe does play a significant role in the push-off phase, you must allow the other toes to assist. Let the big toe remain in the extended position so you can isolate the movement of plantar flexion for the other toes. You will also feel the extensor hallucis longus working to maintain the extension of the big toe. Remember that in most technique classes you might not do enough to build extra strength in various parts of your body. There is no progressive resistance in a technique class. While you may execute enough relevés in one class to strengthen your gastrocnemius, it may not be enough for the toe flexors or extensors.

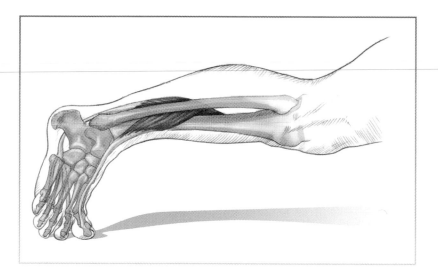

Ankle Dorsiflexion

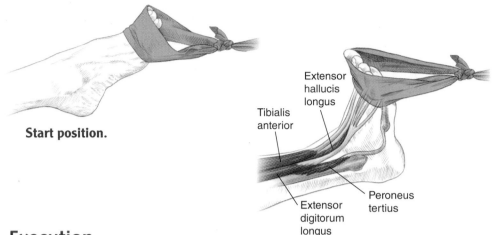

Start position.

Extensor
hallucis
longus

Tibialis
anterior

Peroneus
tertius

Extensor
digitorum
longus

Execution

1. Sit with a resistance band wrapped around your forefoot. Secure the other end to a stable base in front of you. Begin with the ankle in a softly pointed position; the band must be taut at the start of the exercise.

2. Lift the toes against the resistance of the band and continue to increase the resistance by flexing the ankle. Focus on the muscles of the anterior tibia contracting and the posterior tibia lengthening.

3. Hold the contraction for 2 to 4 counts and slowly return to the starting position. Maintain tautness of the band throughout the entire range of motion. Repeat 15 to 30 times, working up to 2 or 3 sets.

⚠️**SAFETY TIP** To avoid sickling or winging of the foot, focus on a neutral position of the ankle, aligning the second toe with the tibia.

Muscles Involved

Tibialis anterior, extensor digitorum longus, extensor hallucis longus, peroneus tertius

Dance Focus

Keeping the front of the tibia bone strong gives you more security when having to dance or turn on your heels. Your warm-up includes a significant amount of relevé and pointing the toes but probably doesn't include rocking back on your heels, which some choreographers may want. The muscles in the back of your lower legs are getting more work than the muscles along the front. This imbalance can create overuse injuries and can hold your technique back. More strength along the front of the tibia bone may also reduce the risk of shin splints. Every grande plié you execute requires contraction of the tibialis anterior muscle to support your tibia bone. This muscle also works to transfer your weight forward to prepare for relevé and helps to maintain a nice lift in your arch. Don't forget about it in your conditioning schedule.

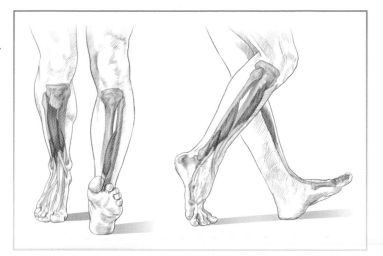

Ball Dorsiflexion

1. Sit on a table and rest your foot on the top of a stability ball. Slowly begin to push the ball forward as the ankle moves into plantar flexion.

2. Allow the foot to point as it stays on top of the ball. You may feel a gentle stretch along the top of the ankle. Push the ball as far you can while keeping the toes lengthened and in contact with the ball. Hold that position for 2 to 4 counts.

3. Slowly begin to reverse the movement, pulling the ankle back into dorsiflexion while pressing the heel down. Lengthen through the Achilles and contract the tibialis anterior. Alternate plantar flexion and dorsiflexion with the assistance of the ball at least 15 times. You can decrease the size of the ball to make the exercise more challenging.

Start position.

Finish position.

WHOLE-BODY TRAINING FOR DANCERS

The field of dance anatomy and research has experienced enormous growth, which is inspiring for those devoted to the field. Excellent dance medicine specialists are located throughout the world, and their passion for helping dancers continues to grow. But the real value in this development benefits you, whether you are a dancer or a teacher. Ongoing research published in medical journals gives dance medicine specialists information to assist you. For example, studies have shown that if you incorporate simple hip flexor conditioning exercises into your daily routine, you can improve the height of your développé. Research also concludes that overuse of the quadriceps with faulty turnout can lead to knee pain and injury. Integrating dance-specific exercises into your training will enhance performance and decrease risks of injury.

Improvement in arabesque could be as simple as strengthening the abdominals and hip extensor muscles while improving movement of the thoracic spine. Improving turnout could be as simple as understanding good neutral pelvic alignment while activating the true hip rotators. By incorporating the principles of body placement, you could improve coordination. When your muscles and bones are more aligned, you actually need less overall muscle action! Therefore, you can perform dance movements without straining and overusing muscles.

Small Props

The exercises in this chapter review musculature previously discussed but use props for added resistance. Dance class uses your own body weight for resistance; this might not be enough effort to truly increase your strength. You will need to go beyond the training offered in dance class. By adding small apparatus and resistance tools, you can build strength beyond the limits of gravity, vary your conditioning plan, and challenge your balance skills. Resistance bands and free weights have already been introduced, but you can use other props to improve technique and keep your training interesting.

Performing exercises on a stability ball, minitrampoline, or rotating discs will increase your body awareness (proprioception). These small props make the exercises more challenging. Challenging your balance in more extreme ways can improve overall balance by transferring the sensations to your dance experiences.

You are able to maintain balance from three sources: visual input from your eyes, sensory receptors of the inner ear, and receptors in the muscles and joints that help postural control. Anytime you try to maintain your balance on an uneven or unstable surface, you challenge your sensory receptors to work harder. To advance any of the exercises throughout this book, close your eyes at various times to focus on integration of mind and body. Have you ever lost your balance when the stage lights suddenly change or go to a blackout? Do you notice how your balance is weak after an injury? Adolescent growth spurts can compromise balance as well as cause fatigue. Any abrupt changes in your sensory systems will weaken proprioception. Training your balance skills will improve acuity and precision of movement.

Training Specifics

If you're concerned about fitting all of these exercises into your busy schedule, focus on a few exercises at a time and slowly incorporate a few into your warm-up and others into your cool-down. Try taking one concept at a time, work on it for a week, then gradually add in another. Execute several exercises from the first four chapters every other day and the extremity exercises on alternating days. Use the exercises to make positive changes in the way you work.

1. Organize your thoughts to perform each exercise with efficiency. Alignment is essential for precision of movement; it is a whole-body sensation. Continue to visualize each movement of your dancing along the various planes of your body. Notice how you can gradually change poor habits and improve your lines.

2. Maintain spinal stability while releasing unnecessary tension. Improve your lung capacity by incorporating good breathing patterns while dancing. Deeper breathing enhances core control and supports moving from your center. Imagine your breath reaching every muscle in your body to enhance every movement.

3. Improvement in proprioception includes mind–body integration while advancing the functional work. Maintain balance awareness while the base of support changes during various floor exercises. Continue to focus on postural awareness while moving from the floor to the barre and into center. Imagine your new balance skills working while you're turning, jumping, and balancing in relevé.

4. To gain muscular strength, warm up your body and repeat exercises to fatigue without compromising alignment. You can increase repetitions or increase resistance, but vary your speed to correlate with changing dance tempos. Practice your favorite dance steps with the same attack and vigor. Repeat basic jump variations to focus more on controlling the landing. Increase the number of repetitions to improve your cardiorespiratory endurance. To avoid faulty compensations, focus on the muscle group creating the movement.

Dance-Focused Exercise

The following exercises are full of challenges. You will add props and more full-body, functional movement. Imagine applying the principles of each exercise to your specific dance style. Memorize the correct desired movement for the best results. You are taking your work to the next level, increasing the challenges for the core and your balance.

Your mind is a powerful tool. Be selective with what you focus on. Quiet your mind so that you can concentrate on the specific area of the body you are working. Before each exercise, zero in on the starting position and movement execution while maintaining a feeling of ease. Speak to yourself using only positive reinforcement! Keep the flow of mental talk inspiring and optimistic.

Wall Plié

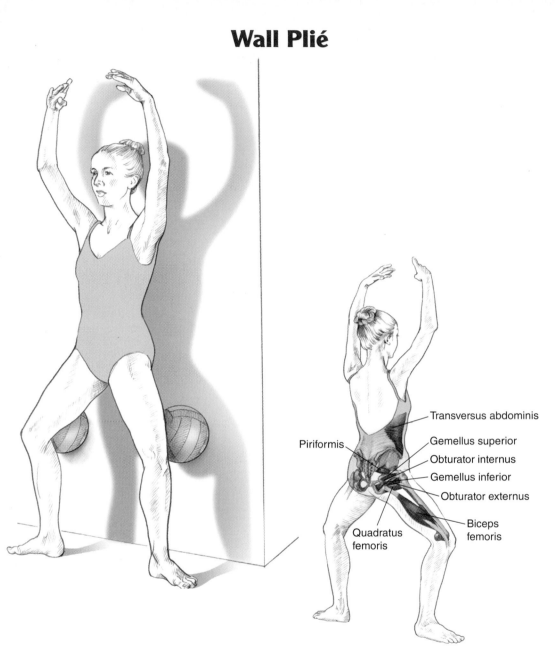

Transversus abdominis

Piriformis

Gemellus superior

Obturator internus

Gemellus inferior

Obturator externus

Biceps femoris

Quadratus femoris

Execution

1. Place your back against the wall. Turn out your legs and place your feet wider than your hips (feet are aligned according to what your turnout allows). Place a ball between each thigh and the wall. Inhale to prepare and maintain a neutral spine and pelvis.

2. On exhalation, press your thighs into the balls by contracting the deep rotators. Focus on maintaining a neutral pelvis. Align the femurs over the midtalus and second metatarsals and hold for 2 to 4 counts. Repeat 8 times.

Muscles Involved

Transversus abdominis, biceps femoris, piriformis, gemellus superior, gemellus inferior, obturator internus, obturator externus, quadratus femoris

Dance Focus

Ease in the hips without straining through the trunk allows for a better turnout. Use the wall plié exercise to focus on the deep hip rotators while maintaining a neutral and secure position of the pelvis. Memorize the feeling of true external rotation in the hip without overuse of the sartorius or lateral thigh or tilting of the pelvis. Focus on alignment of the femur over the second toe; avoid any torque throughout the knee. The long line of the tibia should be placed directly over the center of your foot. Close your eyes for a moment and visualize the deep external obturator as it contracts and pulls the femur outward to increase the turnout. Now relax the rotators. Repeat the detail of the contraction again until you feel how firm and supportive this 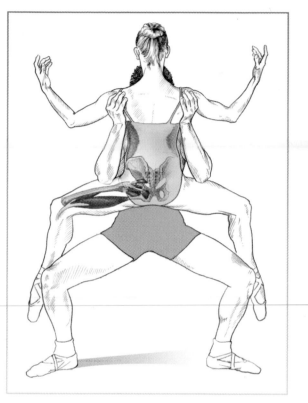 muscle is in rotating your thigh outward. It's important to reemphasize hip disassociation: Let the movement occur in the hip joint so the thighs open into external rotation while the pelvis and spine are stable.

Side Bend With Resistance

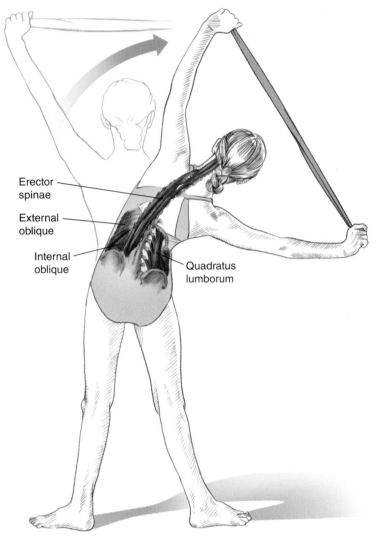

Erector spinae

External oblique

Internal oblique

Quadratus lumborum

Execution

1. Stand firm and steady with legs in second position. Hold the ends of a resistance band in each hand overhead. Feel the weight of the arms traveling down to your scapulae, and widen the arms enough to provide challenging resistance throughout the exercise.

2. As you begin to inhale, lift and lengthen through the spine. Move along your frontal plane and bend directly to the right side. Glide the right scapula downward. Maintain firm resistance with the band. Hold as you exhale.

3. Flex the left ankle and feel lengthening along that leg. Focus on the left heel and thigh working together to maintain turnout along the leg. Reach the left sit bone to the floor. Inhale to return. Repeat 8 times on each side.

Maintain your neutral body placement to avoid anterior pelvic tilt, and work to avoid twisting in the knees.

Muscles Involved

Internal oblique, external oblique, quadratus lumborum, erector spinae

Dance Focus

Because of the lack of flexibility along the thoracic spine, a side bend can be challenging. The rule of axial elongation applies throughout the entire length of the movement. This will create more height along the spinal column to increase motion while your head balances with ease on top. Feel as though you are moving every vertebra separately to achieve a more flexible but secure spine. Any side bend should create a long, lifted arch for aesthetics and for injury prevention. Lengthening along your spine provides for more space between the vertebrae and less compression on the discs. Moving directly along your frontal plane for each cambré side or side tilt movement will be more efficient and aesthetically pleasing than if you moved on a diagonal plane. Awakening the lateral breath movement will give your spine a flexible but secure quality. Your pelvis should feel anchored to resist the trunk's upward pull. Toward the comple-

tion of the side bend, the lower rib cage needs to have a lifted quality as well. Visualize a half moon and imagine soaring sideways!

Diagonal Twist

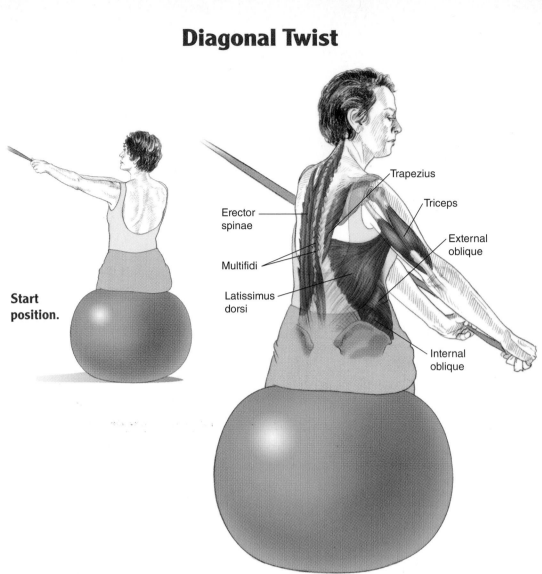

Start position.

Trapezius

Triceps

External oblique

Erector spinae

Multifidi

Latissimus dorsi

Internal oblique

Execution

1. Sit on a stability ball with hips and knees flexed at 90 degrees and feet on the floor. Wrap a resistance band high over the left shoulder; both hands hold the ends. Your pelvis remains neutral on the stability ball while your trunk rotates to the left. Hands holding the resistance band remain aligned with your sternum. Inhale to prepare.

2. On exhalation, engage the deep abdominals, obliques, and scapular stabilizers to rotate your trunk to the right. The arms pull against the resistance of the band in a downward right diagonal pattern.

3. Hold this position for 2 to 4 counts. Feel the oblique musculature working to support your center. Maintain alignment of the hands and extended elbows with the sternum. Return slowly with inhalation. Repeat 6 to 8 times on each side.

SAFETY TIP Avoid twisting and instability in the lower back by maintaining awareness of deep abdominal contraction to support the spine.

Muscles Involved

Latissimus dorsi, lower trapezius, triceps brachii, internal oblique, external oblique, erector spinae, multifidi

Dance Focus

Coordinating strength in rotational and spiraling movements requires strength in the core and deep spine. To allow for more rotation, release tension in the neck and shoulders before the spiral occurs. Remember to engage the lower abdominals to secure the lower spine. This will also allow for more rotation. The diagonal twist is wonderful for the ballroom dancer who has been practicing for hours in upper-back extension and left trunk rotation. Remember the obliques are working for you on both sides; the internal oblique is contracting on the same side as the rotation, while the external oblique is contracting on the opposite side. The same muscle assistance applies with the deep erector spinae muscles: While muscles contract to produce movement

on one side, you also have muscles contracting on the opposite side. This reinforces the need to move from your center; you have to initiate spiral movement from deep in the core and close to the spine.

High Kick With Resistance

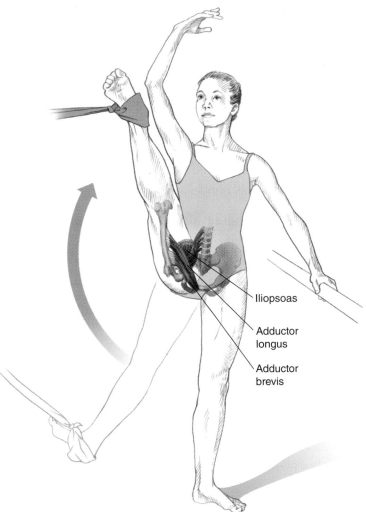

Iliopsoas

Adductor longus

Adductor brevis

Execution

1. Begin with the left hand on the barre and the right leg in a turned-out tendu position to the side. Tie one end of a resistance band around the ankle of the right leg and the other end to an immovable object to the side. Reorganize your neutral placement. Secure the turned-out supporting leg by engaging the gluteus medius.

2. Bring the leg quickly through first position and cross through fifth into a battement devant against the resistance of the band holding firmly along the outside. Coordinate your breathing so that you inhale as the leg goes up.

3. Initiate the movement from the core and inner thighs in the low range. Use the brush through first to fifth to emphasize hip adduction, then engage the iliopsoas as soon as possible to elevate the leg. Return slowly with control.

4. Lengthen through the spine and quadratus lumborum. Maintain turn-out throughout the entire exercise and repeat 4 times; then repeat 4 more times without the resistance.

⚠️ **SAFETY TIP** Avoid lateral hip hike. The trunk muscles want to pull your pelvis upward. Anchor your pelvis. Move the thigh, not the pelvis.

Muscles Involved

Adductor longus, adductor brevis (low level), iliopsoas (higher level)

Dance Focus

Lifting the legs with ease and grace means no extra adjustments, unnecessary weight shift, or overuse of the quadriceps. Working effectively the first time reduces the risk of injury and improves your technique. The higher your leg goes, the harder the deep iliopsoas must contract. Keep working to maintain turnout as much as you can. When the working leg begins to turn in, the anterior fibers of the gluteus minimus and medius begin to take over and will elevate your hip. Visualize the attachment of the iliopsoas on the inside of the femur. Initiate the movement from that area of the thigh and let your leg float up to your chest. With each leg

lift, lengthen the hamstrings, buttocks, and lower-spine musculature. Train your inhalation to help elevate your leg and your exhalation to secure your spine as the leg lowers. Your legs *can* fly!

Attitude on Disc

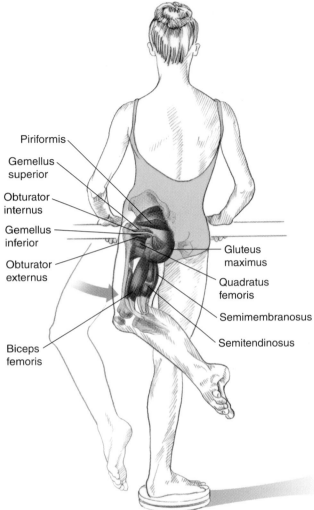

Piriformis

Gemellus superior

Obturator internus

Gemellus inferior

Obturator externus

Biceps femoris

Gluteus maximus

Quadratus femoris

Semimembranosus

Semitendinosus

Execution

1. Face the barre with the right leg turned out on a disc. Your left leg is in coupé position. Organize your placement and balance.

2. Coordinate inhalation with hip extension, moving from coupé to attitude derrière. As the leg elevates, there must be a slight accommodating forward shift of your body. Reemphasize the deep rotators turning out the attitude derrière leg. Engage your deep abdominals to support the lower spine. Lengthen the thoracic spine into a long arch.

3. Hold for 2 to 4 counts, focusing on the gluteus maximus and hamstrings. With exhalation and control, reverse the movement to return to coupé. Repeat 8 times on each side.

SAFETY TIP **Protect your lower spine by engaging the deep abdominals.**

Muscles Involved

Piriformis, gemellus superior, gemellus inferior, obturator internus, obturator externus, quadratus femoris, gluteus maximus, biceps femoris, semitendinosus, semimembranosus

Dance Focus

Initiating extension to the back with the muscles that are primarily responsible for that movement will improve the quality of your technique. Your arabesques will improve when you can protect your lower spine and develop more strength in the hamstrings and gluteus maximus. Practice moving your leg to the back and see how far your leg will go before your lower spine moves. You might be capable of only 15 degrees of movement; in that case, shift forward slightly to accommodate but continue to lift the leg from the hamstrings and gluteus maximus contraction. Whether you are moving into a low attitude or a full arabesque, engage the abdomen to support your spine. Incorporate more movement along your thoracic spine. As you maintain a strong lift in the abdomen, visualize the vertebrae in your midback moving into extension. You have more movement capabilities in the upper back and chest area than you think. It's not about only arching your lower back. Use

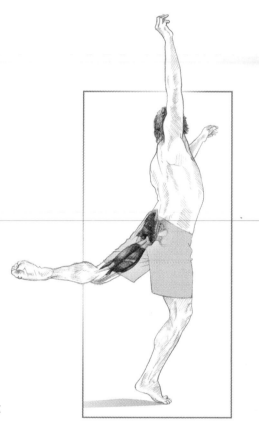

the deep turnout muscles to avoid twisting in the pelvis. Remember your spine is elongated and moving in the longest possible arch. Coordination and beautiful alignment will also reduce tension in the neck and shoulders.

Plank and Pike

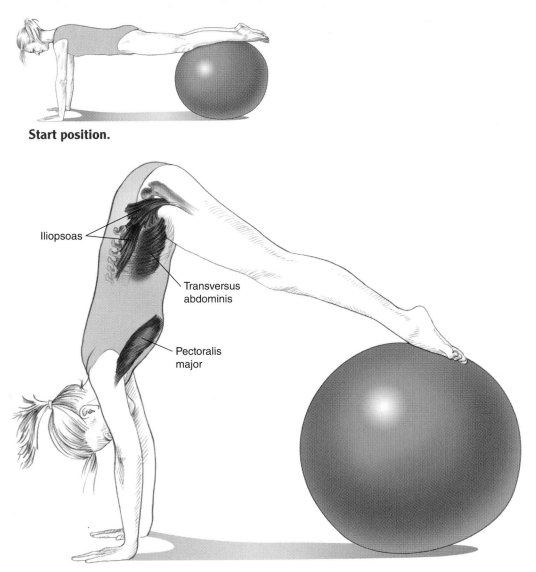

Start position.

Iliopsoas

Transversus
abdominis

Pectoralis
major

Execution

1. Lay the front of your trunk over a stability ball. Walk your hands out until you reach a plank position with the tibias resting on top of the ball. Knees are straight and elbows are straight but not locked. Engage the scapular stabilizers and all trunk stabilizers.

2. On inhalation, initiate the movement with a slight posterior tilt as well as a deep abdominal and hip flexor contraction to elevate your hips into a pike. Lengthen through your spine as you pull the ball toward your chest, pointing your feet.

3. Hold this position for 2 to 4 counts with inhalation. Reemphasize scapular depression and adduction. Slowly return to the beginning plank position with exhalation. Hold the trunk firm to protect your spine. Repeat 6 to 8 times.

⚠️ **SAFETY TIP** Maintain scapular stability. Avoid winging of the scapula. Engage the deep abdominals to resist gravity pulling your spine into extension.

Muscles Involved

Transversus abdominis, iliopsoas, pectoralis major, anterior deltoid

Dance Focus

Some of the most captivating and challenging choreography comes from dancing on the hands. That might mean cartwheels, back handsprings, push-ups, or falling on one hand. Regardless of the movement, you must be prepared and strong. Most dance technique classes won't work your upper body and core sufficiently; it is up to you to put it all together. The plank and pike is a fully integrated mind-to-body skill. The small postural muscles close to your spine as well as your larger muscles contract. Awaken your breathing skills to assist with any movement of this kind. Practice deep lateral inhalation

to prepare yourself and forced exhalation on the movement to support yourself. But if you find yourself losing stability in the lower back, increase your lower-abdominal training. If you find you are unable to maintain stability with the scapulae, increase your shoulder exercises. Choreography that uses plank-type poses is challenging and risky if you are weak. Conditioning will give you a powerful, accomplished look.

Bounding

Trapezius

Rhomboid

Pectoralis major

Start position.

Serratus anterior

Anterior deltoid

Finish position.

Execution

1. Begin in a classic push-up position with hands wider than shoulder width on a minitramp. Legs are extended and feet are on the floor. Reorganize your trunk for core control. You can also begin with knees on the floor.

2. While breathing comfortably, bend the elbows with control to initiate a push-up. Maintain scapular stability.

3. Press into the tramp and push into the air, returning with control. Repeat 6 to 8 times.

Maintain lower-back stability with trunk control. Maintain scapular control and engage the wrist flexors to avoid hyperextension of the wrists.

Muscles Involved

Pectoralis major, anterior deltoid, serratus anterior, lower trapezius, rhomboid

Dance Focus

This rebounding exercise is an excellent way to challenge your core and shoulders to execute almost any tricky choreography. This is also an excellent exercise for dynamic stability. Bounding on the trampoline is another form of resistance training. Your muscles lengthen under the load in the down phase (which is the eccentric contraction), followed by a quick, strong concentric contraction to push you into the air. This combination can help you develop greater muscular power. The controlled falls made so famous by the Graham technique would seem effortless with greater muscular power. All fall-and-recover movements in jazz styles would require less tension if you had greater muscular power. Training safely with organized rebounding-type exercises will prepare you for the complexity of atypical choreographic falls.

Airplane Balance

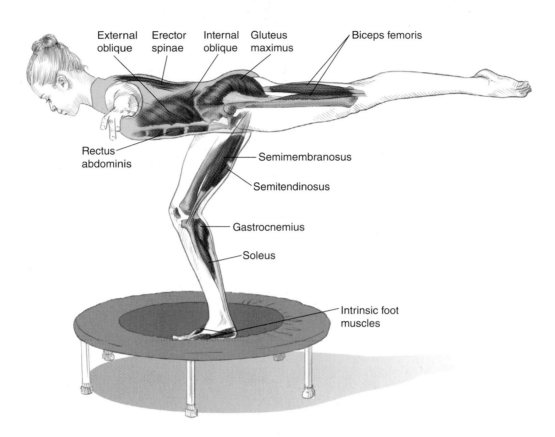

External oblique   Erector spinae   Internal oblique   Gluteus maximus   Biceps femoris

Rectus abdominis

Semimembranosus

Semitendinosus

Gastrocnemius

Soleus

Intrinsic foot muscles

Execution

1. Stand in the middle of the minitramp on one leg in parallel position. The other leg is in parallel arabesque. Lengthen along your spine and move into a flat-back position. Bring your arms out to the side.

2. Organize your balance skills and place your weight between the ball of the foot and the heel. Using the intrinsic muscles of your foot, add a small demi-plié.

3. Maintain your balance for 10 to 30 seconds. Rest and repeat on each side 3 times. Breathe comfortably. Release tension in the neck and shoulders. Use abdominal control and the principle of axial elongation.

Muscles Involved

Rectus abdominis, internal oblique, external oblique, erector spinae

> **Standing leg:** Intrinsic foot muscles, gastrocnemius, soleus, semimembranosus, semitendinosus, gluteus maximus, gluteus minimus, biceps femoris

> **Arabesque leg:** Semimembranosus, semitendinosus, gluteus maximus, biceps femoris

Dance Focus

Improving balance skills can reduce the risk of injury, relieve unnecessary tension, and improve jumps and turns. Take a little time each day to practice balancing. If you don't have a minitramp, then balance in the sand or on a pillow. Find your center and placement beginning along the arches of your foot. Align your weight over the first and fifth metatarsals and the heel. Feel the deep intrinsics supporting you. Focus on your deep postural muscles along your spine and down the leg. When you are truly balanced, you will actually need less muscular effort, which means more efficient work. Breathe comfortably through the balancing process. Let your breathing quiet your center and release tension. Gather your thoughts and organize your body to maintain a healthy balance between body, mind, and spirit.

Parallel Dégagé

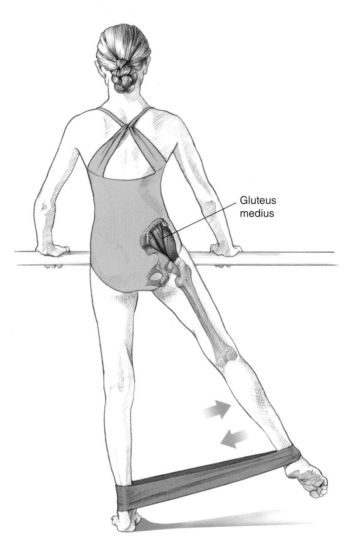

Gluteus medius

Execution

1. Stand with your legs parallel. Loop an elastic band around both ankles and rest both hands on the barre.

2. Breathing comfortably, begin to move your gesture leg in a series of parallel dégagés against the resistance of the band.

3. Maintain your stable neutral position by lifting from the waist and holding your pelvis steady and firm. Feel the gluteus medius of the gesture leg working against the resistance of the band and the gluteus medius of the supporting leg helping you maintain a secure pelvis.

4. Begin with 8 to 10 repetitions on each leg. Work up to 3 full sets.

Muscles Involved

Gluteus medius

Dance Focus

Remember, in order to truly gain strength you must add resistance training to your conditioning program. Pelvic stability is another key to improving posture and technique. Let this exercise help you get in tune with the outside of your pelvis to assist you in gaining strength. The gluteus medius will help you on the supporting leg with développé and grande battement work. The gluteus medius also will help your gesture leg during all side layout positions, traveling steps to the side, and jumping combinations. For added pelvic stability, feel the lengthening along the spine and squeeze the buttocks together. Focus on separating your thigh from your lower back, which will want to move. Feel solid all the way down the supporting leg. As you increase the number of repetitions, you also will feel the work along the hips of the supporting leg and the gesture leg.

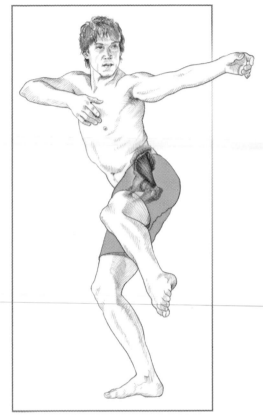

Although the gluteus medius is the main muscle worked, this exercise engages the whole body due to its focus on stability.

EXERCISE FINDER

SPINE

Locating Neutral 20
Leg Glide 22
Trunk Curl Isometrics 24
Hip Flexor Isometrics 26
Spinal Brace 28
Ischial Squeeze 30

RIBS AND BREATH

Lateral Breathing 40
Breathing With Side Bend 42
Breathing With Port de Bras 44
Thoracic Extension 46
Breathing Plié 48

CORE

Side Bend 58
Trunk Curl 60
Oblique Lift 62
Side Lift 64
Coccyx Balance 66
Modified Swan 68
Trunk Twist 70

SHOULDER GIRDLE AND ARMS

External and Internal Rotation 82
Wall Press 84
Port de Bras 86
Biceps Curl 88
Triceps Pull 90

Vs 92

Rowing. 94

Plank 96

Reverse Plank 98

PELVIS AND HIPS

Plié Heel Squeeze 108

Coupé Turn-In 110

Passé Press 112

Inner-Thigh Press 114

Arabesque Prep 116

Hip Flexor Pulse 118

Attitude Lift 120

Hip Flexor Stretch 122

LEGS

Short Arcs. 130

Wall Sit. 132

Hamstring Curl 134

Hamstring Lift. 136

Side Scissor. 138

Assisted Développé. 140

Descending Battement 142

ANKLES AND FEET

Doming 152

Big-Toe Abduction 154

Inversion Press 156

Winging 158

Relevé With Ball 160

Seated Soleus Pump 162

Toe Isolations 164

Ankle Dorsiflexion 166

WHOLE BODY

Wall Plié 172

Side Bend With Resistance 174

Diagonal Twist 176

High Kick With Resistance 178

Attitude on Disc 180

Plank and Pike 182

Bounding 184

Airplane Balance 186

Parallel Dégagé 188

ABOUT THE AUTHOR

Jacqui Greene Haas has been the athletic trainer for the Cincinnati Ballet since 1989, is the director of dance medicine academic seminars (www. dancemedicine.net), and is the director of the dance medicine division of Wellington Orthopedics in Cincinnati, Ohio, where she treats dancers in physical therapy, postsurgical rehabilitation, and general conditioning.

A former professional ballet dancer with Boston Ballet, Southern Ballet Theatre, Tampa Ballet, New Orleans Ballet, and Cincinnati Ballet, Jacqui holds a BA in dance from the University of South Florida and an athletic training certificate from the University of Cincinnati. She also has a certificate in Pilates instruction from St. Francis Memorial Hospital dance division in San Francisco and a certificate in Pilates rehabilitation from Polestar Education in Miami, Florida. She has developed injury-prevention programs for numerous dance studios as well as the McGing Irish Dancers, the School for Creative and Performing Arts, and the University of Cincinnati dance department.

Jacqui is a frequent presenter, speaking to dancers, instructors, and health care practitioners, including presentations at the International Association of Dance Medicine and Science and the National Athletic Trainers' Association conferences. She has been published in *Dance* magazine and *Advance Rehabilitation* magazine.

ANATOMY SERIES

Each book in the *Anatomy Series* provides detailed, full-color anatomical illustrations of the muscles in action and step-by-step instructions that detail perfect technique and form for each pose, exercise, movement, stretch, and stroke.

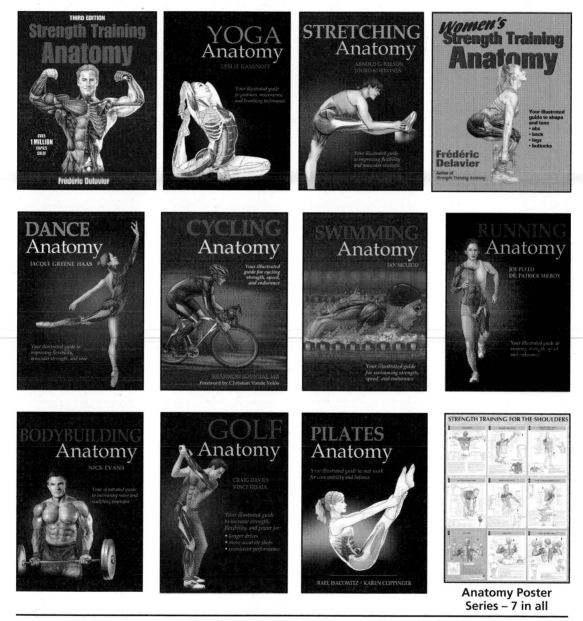

Anatomy Poster Series – 7 in all

To place your order, U.S. customers call TOLL FREE **1-800-747-4457**
In Canada call 1-800-465-7301 • In Europe call +44 (0) 113 255 5665 • In Australia call 08 8372 0999
In New Zealand call 0800 222 062 • or visit **www.HumanKinetics.com/Anatomy**

HUMAN KINETICS
The Premier Publisher for Sports & Fitness
P.O. Box 5076, Champaign, IL 61825-5076